Keith –

Thanks for y[our] support. Here's to yo[ur] continued success. –

[signature]

Acclaim for Greg Bustin and
Lead the Way: Charting a Course to Win

"Lead The Way is full of proven strategies to plan, organize, lead – and make every minute of your day more productive."

Kip Tindell, Chairman and CEO, The Container Store

"In his new book *Lead The Way*, Greg Bustin makes a compelling case for developing a written plan for your business, and then in a very readable and understandable way tells you how you can develop and create ownership of the execution of an outstanding plan. Compelling reading for anyone leading an enterprise who wants to be an effective leader."

Richard Carr, Vice Chairman of the Board, Vistage International

"Greg nails this one! This book is a practical tool for getting your team informed, aligned and motivated. Unlike long stories and fables, this book leaves the business jargon behind and provides pure protein to readers. Greg has put so much into this book it's like reading a dozen books at once. I can't wait to share with my team tomorrow. For those who have never had a strategic plan, it's a must do!"

Jeff Bowling, CEO, The Delta Companies

"Greg provides an effective blueprint for any business seeking to separate itself from the pack. Moving beyond books that seek solely to inspire, Greg provides a concise, practical guide along with proven processes that prompt leaders to ask critical questions and challenge themselves to improve individual and organizational performance."

**David E. Alexander, Vice Chair and Southwest
Area Managing Partner, Ernst & Young LLP**

"Greg Bustin has written a valuable book against which a CEO or senior leader can compare his or her organization's planning process. Greg offers a very thorough step-by-step process for planning, for gaining insight and follow-through which will lead to an organization's success."

Ebby Halliday, Chairman, Ebby Halliday REALTORS

"*Lead The Way* is a must read for CEOs that want to play at the top of their game. Greg lays it all out in a step-by-step process to help leadership teams develop, execute and measure winning performance."

Bob Nichol, CEO, Southwest Media Group

"The biggest problem that most smaller businesses have is they don't have a plan. Greg's book makes the crucial step of developing a plan much easier and productive for a CEO. Greg keeps it simple – which is exactly as it should be."

Mike Rawlings, Managing Partner, CIC Partners,
and former President of Pizza Hut

"Consistent success doesn't have to be elusive. After years of helping leaders produce results for their organizations, Greg opens his playbook for busy CEOs. And it works! His practical approach makes the hard work of planning and execution straightforward and rewarding."

Ernest Z. Frausto, President, Nest Entertainment

"Winning organizations and individuals are pioneers that lead the way by continuously improving the products and services they offer their customers. Greg Bustin's book is all about discovering what works and then staying focused on implementing it. We've certainly benefited from Greg's expertise in this area."

Luis Davila, General Manager, Pella Corporation

"Greg's years of experience is demonstrated in this practical, action-oriented, specific how-to book – including details of the planning process through implementation and monitoring. His passionate emphasis on gaining commitment and accountability sets a standard on achieving alignment and accomplishing the important objectives as a result of the planning process. *Lead the Way* is filled with real life examples that can help improve results in any environment."

Ed Bowman, CEO, SOURCECORP, Incorporated

"Greg's book inspires action because it helps leaders see their plan more clearly and understand how best to bring their people along with them. His book is like a magnificent golf course and each chapter is like playing one spectacular hole after another – it is inspiring and motivating. I recommend having a pad and pen handy – I have notes on every page."

Reed Melnick, CEO, Nevill Business Solutions

"I've participated in four other strategic planning sessions, and have always come away disappointed. Greg's approach to planning engaged our team and has changed our company for the better. Our team now knows the goals, what it takes to accomplish them and is committed to achieving them. We've outperformed our best year by 250% as a result of a better focus on execution. I'm a big fan of Greg's."

Jerry Smith, CEO, Integrity Integration Resources

"I have seen Greg in action. Greg reminds leaders and staff alike that the fundamentals of business are just that: fundamental. Ignoring Greg's advice in favor of the latest fad is dangerous to your business or your career. Implement the approaches he recommends and watch your part of the business world become a winner."

Len Suazo, Chief Operating Officer, Metro Label

"Greg helped lead a strategic planning initiative in our church and was able to challenge long-held beliefs in a collaborative effort that allowed everyone involved to feel ownership in the process and in the resulting plan. We are now reaping the benefits of this planning effort, and Greg's leadership and counsel throughout have made us better as individuals and as a congregation."

John Jenkins, Partner, Macfarlan Capital Partners

"Greg's process creates a safe environment where important, difficult issues affecting the organization's performance can be discussed. Everyone knows what those issues are, but it can be hard to talk about them because of egos, feelings and attitudes. Greg's approach to planning helps us talk about it in a non-threatening way in order to dissect the tough issues and then go to work on them as a team."

Kyle Ulam, COO, Integrity Integration Resources

"We've worked with Greg on a number of occasions, and he always delivers meaningful content in a positive style that engages our team to think differently about the value we deliver to our customers."

**Ray Napolitan, President, American Building Systems
and Vice President, Nucor Corp.**

"Greg Bustin helped our management team develop a 5-year strategic and operational plan. While I had some product questions and operational issues that I wanted to address, and we did, the planning sessions went much further because of Greg's planning process and experience."

Dan O'Hara, CEO, Universal Conversion Technologies

"We hired Greg to help us because of his obvious professional credentials and experience. His proactive approach and grass roots style ensured that every employee was included in the process and took ownership in our new plan."

Scott Metko, CEO, Starfire

"After engaging Greg Bustin to facilitate our company-wide strategic planning session, our team came away enthused, energized and totally focused on their goals and how to achieve them. It was a career-changing session for many of them. Greg is a dynamic facilitator who does a great job of keeping people on task, on time and focused on the most significant issues."

Gregg Imlach, CEO, Imlach Group

"Greg Bustin outlines a total no-nonsense approach to strategic planning through a step by step guide that's pragmatic and easy to implement. He boils down the best practices of strategic planning into manageable tasks that can deliver tangible results in a two-day session."

Lisa Blackburn, Principal, The Structure Group

"Greg Bustin challenged our team to rethink our goal setting process and prompted us to ask key questions we had not previously considered. We now have a tighter planning process, more team alignment and ultimately more focus as a company."

Greg Boyd, President, MIS Group

"Greg reinforces the principle that there are no shortcuts to planning and execution. Quality time invested in developing, communicating and implementing a plan helps turn good companies into great ones."

Don Clampitt, CEO, Clampitt Paper

"Greg's planning process helped a group of professionals from various backgrounds and different perspectives agree on the major areas we needed to focus on to achieve our desired outcomes. The simplicity and clarity about our mission, our vision and the key strategies and action items for moving forward have already provided faster and better implementation results than the strategic plan developed five years ago."

John Palms, CEO, Bibbentucker's

"We all know, intuitively and intellectually, that planning is the catalyst to excellence in every endeavor. Greg Bustin, with his well-crafted insights, provides the tools to leverage the planning process – through meaningful interaction, collaboration and thought-provoking tools – into measurable results."

Bruce Bradford, North Texas Regional CEO, Sterling Bank

"If you want to improve your company's effectiveness, this book provides the blueprint. Time is short so using this comprehensive guide is the most efficient way to accomplish your purpose. Greg has written a book that bears reading more than once, perhaps even periodically, because it provides the catalyst for business leaders to do the thinking they can do but don't always get around to except when being challenged and guided by a book such as this."

Ron Farmer, CEO, US LED, Ltd.

"Greg does a great job taking an organization step-by-step through the planning process, providing straightforward steps, valuable exercises and helpful samples. Just as important, however, he helps leaders appreciate the benefits of introspection. By knowing more about themselves and one another, leaders can use Greg's process to drive results."

Jeff Hook, President and CEO, Fellowship Technologies

"Greg has created an excellent strategic planning and execution tool for leaders who are serious about improving their performance. His book could be called 'The CEO's Survival Handbook' because it's loaded with great information, practical tools and powerful exercises that help leaders and their teams wrestle with change as they move toward success."

Jim Buchanan CEO, Buchanan Associates

Lead the Way

LEAD
THE WAY

Charting A Course To Win

Greg Bustin

Lead the Way: Charting a Course to Win

Front cover design by Greg Chapman

Published by Wheatmark®
610 East Delano Street, Suite 104, Tucson, Arizona 85705 U.S.A.
(888) 934-0888 ext. 3
www.wheatmark.com

ISBN: 978-1-58736-651-2 (paperback)
ISBN: 978-1-58736-652-9 (hardcover)
LCCN: 2007939842

For my two girls – Janet and Jordan

"If you don't know where you are going, any road will get you there."

~ Lewis Carroll

"What lies before us and what lies behind us are small matters compared to what lies within us. And when we bring what is within out into the world, miracles happen."

~ Henry David Thoreau

Contents

"Champions are champions not because they do anything extraordinary but because they do the ordinary things better than anyone else."

~ Chuck Noll

Introduction

As a busy CEO, your most precious commodity is time. There simply isn't enough of it in your day. Occasionally, however, you take time to reflect on the past and look to the future. Then before you know it, you're back in the thick of your business wrestling with obstacles, opportunities and distractions.

Ideas, dreams and goals you contemplated as reasonable possibilities evaporate as the daily grind takes over and new issues emerge. Your star employee wants more money. Your biggest competitor just cut their prices. Your recent growth spurt has placed pressure on cash flow. That huge new business opportunity you spent the past 12 months cultivating is ready to move forward, but you're not sure you have all the necessary people or systems in place to deliver on your promises. Your most important customers have new needs and only you can address them – or so it seems.

Am I running my business or is my business running me? you wonder.

What if you could focus your resources so that both you and your business operate at higher levels of effectiveness?

Wouldn't it follow that a more effective business operation should lead to increased profitability?

Everyone's got the same 24 hours in a day. So how do the most successful CEOs do it?

Whether you're the leader of a business that's in its infancy or the CEO of an established company, this book will help you.

After 25 years of working with and observing hundreds of senior business leaders, I've concluded that what separates those who are most effective from all the rest is their ability to do one thing exceptionally well.

The most successful leaders win consistently because they have a plan that they work.

They work their plan to deliver results effectively and profitably. They make time work for them by getting everyone in the business focused on the right things and performing at consistently high levels of execution.

In my first book, *Take Charge! How Leaders Profit From Change*, I outlined three guiding principles for leading in times of change. Great leaders:

1. Know what they believe – they operate from a set of core values that help them discern right from wrong.

2. Define success on their own terms – in times of change, they buck trends, question premises and try new approaches.

3. Lead the way – they articulate the challenge, explain the importance of what must be done, set the course and instill processes to get the right things done the right way.

It's this third principle that we'll examine at length in this book.

Here's what distinguishes exceptional companies from average performers: leaders who understand the power of reducing the organization's priorities to a concisely written plan that can be embraced by the organization and tracked relentlessly to measure progress against specific priorities.

And there's the challenge. On one hand, a strategically sound plan that maps specific initiatives and improvements will deliver little new value to an organization if there's no follow-through or if things continue to be done the way they've always been done. On the other hand, consistent execution of a flawed strategy can actually accelerate an organization's demise.

To improve performance, organizations require a smart plan that's executed crisply and consistently.

Assuming the idea of a smoother-running, more profitable company is important to you, you'll first need to commit a chunk of time to prepare your company for its self-improvement initiative. I know – this is time that you don't really have. Too bad. As the leader, you cannot delegate this responsibility.

I've heard leaders boast that they can develop a plan in an hour. They probably can. My experience has been that half of planning is intellectual and the other half is emotional. Without across-the-board buy-in, your plan will go nowhere fast. You can accelerate emotional buy-in, but you can't expect to achieve the kind of ownership you'll need to implement your plan without bringing your decision-makers together and giving them a voice in the plan. That takes time. Becoming a consistent winner rarely happens overnight.

I've also seen companies – big and small – take months to develop a plan. You don't have that kind of time, and it's not necessary anyway.

This book will provide you with a step by step path to winning. You may be struck by the simplicity of my process. Don't be fooled. Just because the process is simple doesn't undermine its effectiveness. Rather, its value lies in its simplicity. The entire process is designed specifically to overcome the biggest planning and execution hurdles.

Plans fail in their execution for three primary reasons: they're too complicated, there's little genuine excitement about the plan, and there's only lukewarm commitment to execute it. CEOs say, "Give me a fast, simple process my team will believe in and that will produce bottom-line results." The laser-like approach you'll find in this book uses a series of exercises developed from years of watching and working with hundreds of senior leaders who are committed to improving their companies' results.

With discipline, you can turn your ideas, dreams and plans into improved performance.

- In Part 1, we'll examine opportunities in your company for improvement and get you ready to begin your planning process.

- Part 2 will set you up for your own planning sessions by providing proven steps, models and exercises to develop your plan.

- In Part 3, you'll be off to the races implementing your plan with guidelines and systems for executing your plan, ensuring accountability and generating enthusiasm throughout your organization. We'll examine lessons that America's most admired companies – each starting as a small business – learned about sustaining success and winning year after year.

At the end of each chapter and sections of longer chapters, you'll be challenged to turn your thoughts into action and apply what you've just finished reading.

You're about to invest your most precious commodity to position you and your business to win as you've never won before. Consider it time well spent.

Part 1

*When the leader's work is done,
the people will say "We did it
ourselves."*

~ Lao Tzu

Ready...

"In preparing for battle, I have always found that plans are useless, but planning is indispensable."

~ Dwight D. Eisenhower

1

How's Your Performance?

Y ou wouldn't build a house without a blueprint. Why would you try to build your business without a written plan?

Yet as inevitably as the seasons change, thousands of companies every year shut their doors because of the leadership team's failure to develop a written plan and then implement it. Tens of thousands of other companies fail to reach their full potential for the same reason.

It's true that a poor planning process is a giant distraction and a huge waste of time.

Properly conceived and carried out, planning can help any organization become more effective. The paradox of planning is that the very act of preparing a plan will help you and your team pinpoint significant opportunities for increased effectiveness and profitability even though the chances are good you won't implement your plan as it was developed. This is what makes planning indispensable. (We'll examine other benefits of planning in Chapter 3.)

Why don't more companies develop a plan that they will implement?

It's estimated that four out of five businesses don't operate from a written plan. Most of these are small companies. Yet of

7

those businesses that invest the time to develop a written plan, studies show that only one company in four actually integrates its plan into day-to-day operations.

Do executives believe that preparing a budget is the same thing as preparing a plan? Or are they not sure how to create a plan? Are they intimidated by the process? Or do they believe the idea of planning is a giant time-waster because no single individual really owns what's in the plan? Are they concerned that changing marketplace conditions will render the plan obsolete within weeks of its development?

Yes.

What's more, my experience working with leadership teams supports the findings that the vast majority of businesses today operates without a written plan. If these reasons – excuses, really – are what's stopping you, it's time to take a fresh look at the power of effective planning.

Most of the CEOs of small businesses that I've worked with substitute some form of budgeting for a planning process. Budgeting is a form of planning, but there's more to planning than just crunching numbers as we'll show in Part 2. Other CEOs haven't committed their plans to paper. They believe everyone already knows what to do, so the mandate becomes doing more of the same thing next year.

I also see some confusion between annual planning and strategic planning.

If you've not planned at all or you've had difficultly implementing your plans, your initial approach to planning should be to develop an annual plan. As we'll examine in Part 2, this approach focuses on affirming values and direction, establishing priorities and translating those priorities into specific objectives with supporting action items, responsibilities and deadlines. An annual plan is fairly tactical and operational. Thought must be given to this plan, but its primary value is derived from getting all of your leaders focused on the most important operational issues that they and their teams will implement over the next 12 months to improve performance.

Once you've developed and implemented an annual plan, you and your team can turn your attention in Year 2 to developing and implementing a strategic plan. As we'll examine in Part 3, a strategic plan focuses on determining the new opportunities you should investigate or pursue. *Where are the gaps or opportunities in our product or service offerings? What emerging patterns or trends have we identified that we may be able to capitalize upon? Are there any competitors or up-and-coming businesses that we should look at acquiring?* Strategic planning should examine fresh opportunities that can increase your profitable growth.

First things first.

To get you ready for planning, take a couple of minutes right now to assess your organization's performance and see for yourself where your business is doing well and where it's most vulnerable.

Take Action: A Self-Assessment for Leaders

Circle 5 if your organization consistently conforms to this statement, 3 if it sometimes conforms, and 1 if your organization rarely or never conforms.

Section A

1 2 3 4 5   We do what's right for our customers, employees, suppliers and investors regardless of consequence.

1 2 3 4 5   We are truthful and transparent to everyone, recognizing that the omission of key facts is a lie.

1 2 3 4 5   Our organization treats everyone with respect.

1 2 3 4 5   We praise in public and punish in private.

1 2 3 4 5   We try to understand others' points of view before trying to persuade them to ours.

Subtotal _____

Section B

1 2 3 4 5   Our organization's mission, vision and values are clearly defined and articulated.

1 2 3 4 5   Our organization's direction generates excitement and enthusiasm among everyone.

1 2 3 4 5   Everyone in our organization knows the top objectives and understands what's expected of them.

1 2 3 4 5   We know what makes our firm special and we are relentlessly focused on delivering this value.

1 2 3 4 5   Our leaders agree with where we are and where we're going before we implement any initiative.

Subtotal _____

Section C

1 2 3 4 5   We aspire to the highest levels of excellence in all that we undertake.

1 2 3 4 5   We value the benefits of planning so we take time to plan.

1 2 3 4 5   When planning, we think big, view old problems in new ways, and encourage radical ideas.

1 2 3 4 5   New approaches and initiatives generate excitement and enthusiasm among everyone.

1 2 3 4 5   We put our plans, procedures and policies in writing and make them accessible, as appropriate.

Subtotal _____

Section D

1 2 3 4 5   We base decisions on logical, factual information, and not on emotions.

1 2 3 4 5   We are willing to make decisions based on gathering 80 percent of the data.

1 2 3 4 5   Our organization moves forward with sound ideas, even if those ideas are unpopular.

1 2 3 4 5   When we make a decision, we move forward to implement it.

1 2 3 4 5   We take action to solve problems immediately.

Subtotal _____

Section E

1 2 3 4 5   Though we've been successful consistently, we look regularly at changing what we're doing.

1 2 3 4 5   We do not give in to pressures simply to avoid confrontation.

1 2 3 4 5   Performance matters, so we use processes to measure and reward (or reprimand) performance.

1 2 3 4 5   We have systems in place to replicate successes and minimize failures.

1 2 3 4 5   Our organization will change course when the situation dictates or warrants doing so.

Subtotal _____

Section F

1 2 3 4 5   Our organization follows through on commitments made to customers, employees, suppliers
and investors.

1 2 3 4 5   We take responsibility for our actions and accept
responsibility for our mistakes.

1 2 3 4 5   We consistently meet our objectives within speci-
fied deadlines with no follow-up required.

1 2 3 4 5   We do not allow temporary setbacks to cause us
to abandon our objectives.

1 2 3 4 5   We reward results, not activities.

Subtotal _____

Calculate your total score: _____

Turn to the next chapter to learn what your scores tell you about
your organization – and yourself.

"Drive thy business or it will drive thee."

~ Benjamin Franklin

2

Who's Running Your Business?

To over-simplify, there are two kinds of CEOs:

- Those that think about the future and determine how best to position their organizations to capitalize on emerging trends

- Those that choose to respond or react to events that affect their organizations

Which kind are you?

The most effective CEOs play offense, not defense. They play to win. And they don't play scared.

They operate their companies from a game plan the entire team uses to guide decision-making, replicate successes and correct sub-par performance.

The game plan is a reflection of an operating culture where all employees in the business embrace the company's purpose and are driving toward a target, pushing for more and greater accomplishments. Company-wide goals are visible to all. Each employee knows his or her role in the company and what's expected of them. Progress toward the goal is measured, communicated and recognized.

Without a written game plan, of course, a business can succeed at some level. Often for years. Eventually, however, the lack of unity around a common vision and effective policies, procedures and practices will cause that company to hit a wall in terms of the kind of consistent and profitable performance that's capable of being sustained year after year.

How does this happen? Simple. Your business hits a wall shortly after you hit your own personal wall. When does that occur? When you find yourself turning from one fire to the next personally attending to every significant opportunity or crisis. Why does this happen? Because the structure and guiding direction of a well-thought-out plan to address these issues without your personal involvement is absent. In effect, you force your company to wait until you or the leadership team can create a mini-plan for each issue as the issue arises. You are managing by exception rather than by objective. This means the ability of your company to grow and flourish becomes directly proportional to the amount of work you can personally oversee. Bam. You and your business have just hit a wall. You're out of time, and your company's growth is stunted.

Check out your score to see if you're driving your business – or being driven by it.

135-150 Rating

Congratulations. You operate as an effective leadership team. You are making effective use of resources to deliver excellent results. Keep up the good work and remain vigilant in order to address changing conditions inside and outside your organization that can affect your high levels of effectiveness and profitability.

120-134 Rating

Good work. You are doing a number of important things effectively. Continue to maintain your strengths and examine areas where renewed focus and discipline can deliver the greatest potential to improve your performance.

105-119 Rating

Caution... Your company's effectiveness is being diminished significantly. Leadership issues are hampering your organization's performance. Your scores indicate you are responding to issues rather than moving toward a specific goal. Focus immediately to address the most significant problem areas that indicate your company's operations are at risk.

Here's what your scores mean by section:

Section A – Our culture is based on integrity that is evident to all – inside and outside our organization.

Section B – Our mission and vision are clearly defined and are embraced by everyone in the organization.

Section C – We value the planning process and follow the five principles of effective planning.

Section D – We use systems to gather facts and make decisions, then act decisively to implement our decisions.

Section E – We monitor and measure performance of individuals, departments and the organization as a whole.

Section F – We stand behind our performance and recognize results.

Take Action:

After examining your overall score as well as your scores by section, determine where improving your performance will produce the most significant impact. What single action will you commit to taking in the next 30 days to improve your performance? Write your commitment in the space below.

_____

_____

Note: Most leadership teams that complete this self-assessment commit to rating themselves again to track changes in their performance. An ideal time to re-assess your company's performance is at a planning update session 4 – 8 months after your initial planning session.

"Even if you're on the right track, you'll get run over if you just sit there."

~ Will Rogers

3

What Results Should Planning Deliver?

A successful past does not guarantee a successful future.

So don't consider planning "messing with success." Instead, consider planning an opportunity to develop better and more profitable ways of giving your customers more of what they value on a consistent basis.

That's one of the tangible benefits your planning process should deliver, and there are at least nine other positive results you and your team should expect to reap when you plan for the future. The three most significant results are:

- Achieving alignment among your leadership team

- Uncovering new ideas and new or improved revenue streams and ways to improve profitability

- Determining specific objectives and action items to be implemented

Let's take a look at all of the 10 benefits of effective planning, concluding with the three most important benefits.

Breaks Down Silos

Most people in a company are focused on making things happen in their own world. Each department works on its distinct activities and respective to-do lists. Planning creates the opportunity for all department leaders to come together as a group to examine problems and opportunities from a holistic perspective. This forum gives all leaders the chance to look at things from each other's perspective to construct a more accurate version of reality. Of equal importance, planning provides an opportunity for team members to consider issues from the CEO's perspective. When these shifts in perspective occur, good things happen. Opportunities are explored. Problems are solved. Teamwork grows. Effectiveness improves. A CEO who's a member of an executive think tank I lead says, "None of us is as smart as all of us."

Provides a Safe Harbor for "Possibility Thinking"

Five words prevent an organization from achieving its full potential: *We've never done that before.* Here are six more: *We've always done it this way.* Even your best people are reluctant to offer their ideas on ways to tackle a problem or suggest a new way of making money if they know their comments will be stiff-armed with comments like these. Planning should create an environment where creativity is encouraged, new thinking is expected, and disbelief is temporarily suspended. There's plenty of time later for analysis, reason and judgment to determine if a possibility can become a reality. It's been said that if you can't predict the future, create it. Planning provides a structured way to talk openly about issues, events and scenarios that can occur in the future and bring significant change to your organization. Good and bad. Identifying possible future scenarios is less about predicting the future and more about reframing your view of reality in order to make better decisions in the future. When you plan, make it safe, fun and easy for people to speak up and offer their perspective on what's possible. Don't just ask *Why?*, ask *Why not?*

Motivates Your Team and Increases Their Value

Once you and your team start talking about possibilities, you'll discover a new level of energy in the room. The future can be intimidating or it can be exciting. It's your choice. Good planning processes will make thinking about the future exciting. Not because you're sugar-coating things. Just the opposite: You are raising issues and inviting your leaders to address them. People want to contribute and they want to succeed. Planning provides the blueprint. Every organization can improve. That's a fact. Organizational improvement starts with you and your people. Employees who know what's expected of them will perform more effectively and increase their value to the company. What's more, people will embrace plans they've had a voice in developing. Warning: Nothing will sap the energy of your team quicker than developing a plan and not following through. We'll examine ways to secure buy-in and ensure accountability in Chapter 9.

Exposes Blind Spots

Another way to think about how decisions are made is by considering your blind spots. We all have them. We're simply oblivious to certain people, situations or even our own actions that others see all too clearly or in a completely different light. Planning provides a framework to ask questions and expose blind spots. Socrates used questions to illuminate core truths, and today, the Socratic Method is recognized as one of the most effective forms of getting to the truth – whether it be for a person, a team or an entire organization. "Know thyself," Socrates said, noting that self-knowledge is the starting point of discovery because the greatest source of confusion is the failure to realize how little we know about anything, including ourselves. Chapters 7 and 8 are devoted to questions and exercises that will help you and your team expose your personal and organizational blind spots.

Ensures You're Working on the Right Things Versus Doing Things Right

Don't confuse budgeting with planning. Budgeting is a form of planning, but it has two main drawbacks: 1) it perpetuates the silo thinking that may already exist within your organization as each department or functional area prepares its set of resource requirements; and, 2) a budget-based approach to planning uses your existing budget as a platform to construct next year's plans and financials so there's a tendency to treat planning as little more than filling in numbers in a spreadsheet formula. A budget-based approach brings a mindset that says *The people are in place, other costs are givens, the work's what it is, so here's the number for next year.* I'm exaggerating some, but the point is that such plans are built with little interest shown in questioning the status quo. When approached from a zero-based, anything's possible attitude, planning can drive improvements in your business. Smart companies need budgets, too, but they leverage planning to make sure they're working on the right things, and not just doing things right. This type of planning requires more effort to view all aspects of your operation from a clean-slate perspective. And it forces you to confront realities, which can be uncomfortable. But when done right, this type of approach can be refreshing and rewarding.

Brings Focus, Order and Clarity to Your Business

CEOs are intent on getting things done effectively and improving their bottom-line results. Planning brings clarity and focus to your business by taking a methodical, organized approach to breaking down the components of your business. *Who are our best customers? What are our most significant priorities? What people, process and programs must we have in place to achieve them?* Be specific about what you want and how you'll achieve it.

Plans of any kind – personal or professional – dissolve when goals are abstract or ambiguous and when people don't see that what they're doing today makes a difference toward achieving the goal. A well-run planning process delivers focus, order and clarity.

Establishes Accountability

Leaders I've worked with agree that there's generally no shortage of ideas during the planning process. What's usually missing is follow-through and a lack of accountability. *What guarantee do I have that this plan will work?* they ask me. None, if there's no buy-in from the leadership team. None, if the company – starting at the top – is unwilling to change. None, if there's no discipline and performance is not tracked. None, if there are no rewards and penalties tied to performance. There's a simple yet highly effective tool for establishing accountability during the planning process that we'll examine in Chapter 9.

Uncovers New Ideas, New Revenue Streams and Ways to Improve Performance

Value is determined outside your company by your customers and prospective customers. Use the planning process to identify or confirm your core competency and understand the value the market places on it. If you can't answer "Why us?" don't expect the market to know. Sound scary? It's the truth. The good news is that anyone in your company that visits with customers regularly knows what your customers value most, and the planning process can help you uncover new or more effective ways for giving your customers more of what they want. Use the planning process as a springboard to identify and evaluate new opportunities, consider new strategies and discuss objectives that may at first seem unattainable. Uncovering new opportunities to increase performance is one of the three most significant outcomes to expect at the completion of your planning process.

Achieves Alignment Among Your Leadership Team

Bringing your leadership team together to plan provides every participant with an equal opportunity to provide their perspective on critical issues, organizational priorities and the future vision of the company. And just like a wedding, at the end of the strategic planning process, every participant is invited to "Speak now or forever hold your peace." Lack of alignment among the leadership team will, at the least, hold back your organization and, at worst, kill it. So if there's a lack of alignment following the planning process, it's best to ask those who fundamentally disagree with you to move on then wish them well. Because if senior leaders can't agree on what's to be done and how, by whom and by when, this lack of alignment will trickle down through your organization and dilute or even poison daily operations. Alignment is another of the three most significant outcomes you should expect at the completion of your planning process.

Determines Specific Objectives and Action Items To Be Implemented

At the beginning of the day, it's all about possibilities. At the end of the day, it's all about results. A clear, written plan increases significantly the odds of you and your team achieving your objectives. You and your team will agree on your priorities and develop a written action plan focused on making the right things happen. Your plan needn't be long or complicated to be effective. The shorter the better. I'll share a template for your written plan in Chapter 8 that contributes to accountability and drives results. We'll take a brief look at time management models you can use to increase your own effectiveness. As you begin implementing your plan, use the guidelines established in your planning process to monitor progress, watch for variances and track success. Failure to implement what you have created will make planning, as one CEO said, "an expensive hobby." Your plan should be flexible enough to make adjustments based on changing priorities, accomplishments to date, and changing market conditions. We'll examine in Chapter 11 how four hours each month that's spent tracking your plan's implementation delivers the performance you expect.

There may be other benefits to planning, but these 10 top the list.

Take Action:

List the three benefits or outcomes that are most important for you and your team to gain from your planning process.

1. _____

2. _____

3. _____

"The greater danger for most of us is not that our aim is too high, but that it is too low and we reach it."

~ Michelangelo

4

Getting the Most
Out of Planning

We've discussed the benefits of planning, so let's look at five principles that are essential components for you and your team to extract the full value from your planning process.

Consider these five great truths the foundation not just for planning purposes, but also for the way you run your business and live your life.

Decide How Good You Want To Be

Aim for excellence. The planning process allows you and your team to critique in a constructive manner your organization on an ongoing basis. Often, sustaining excellence requires that you have the courage to "break it and then fix it," because chances are good that what worked before won't work today, much less tomorrow. Whatever your goal, make certain it's clear to everyone. Meanwhile, your company's commitment to high standards and continuous improvement must never waver. Because successful companies know that good enough never is.

Resist Shortcuts

Time is precious. In the next chapter we'll examine a struc-

ture that condenses the crucial components of planning and
accountability into a total of 73 hours. These 73 hours aren't
a shortcut. They're a structured approach to leveraging time
using proven, practical methods to improve your company's
performance. Resisting shortcuts first and foremost means
taking time to plan. Given the territory that must be covered
when you assemble your leadership team to plan, you'll see
that the two full days of planning will fly by. As your team
moves through the planning exercises, avoid the temptation to
skip past old issues in a race to move to new solutions – these
lingering issues often affect future performance. Refrain from
killing a possible solution before it can be fully explored. Resisting shortcuts means avoiding so-called quick fixes that create a false sense of security that substantive results are being
generated when they're not. "We're making things happen,"
some may say. True. But are they the right things? To make certain, think critically about what you're trying to accomplish in
the long run, not just the short term. When you think from this
vantage point, you'll be more effective organizing your business to meet your long-term objectives. Then think about how
long it will realistically take to get to where you want to go
and what other resources besides time will be required. Don't
confuse a sense of urgency with taking harmful shortcuts. Effective CEOs are focused and urgent, but they wisely counsel
patience and resist quick, superficial fixes.

Recalibrate Your Plan but Never Give Up
Persistence is a hallmark of successful CEOs and winning
companies. So when things go wrong as they inevitably will,
remember that how you respond defines both you and your organization. All eyes will be on you. Remain calm, gather your
senior leaders and take the opportunity with them to assess
the situation and learn from it. Maintain your discipline. Stay
focused on your long-term vision. Then recalibrate your plan.
If tough decisions must be made, make them. Never give up on

moving forward to achieve your ultimate goal. You may need a new plan or a new objective. But never give up.

Commit Your Plan to Writing

Committing your plan to writing preserves thinking and allows you and your team to measure performance. You read in the last chapter that a written plan is one of the three most significant outcomes you should expect from a well-run planning process. (The other two are leadership alignment, and uncovering new ideas to improve revenue and profitability.) Talking about what you're going to do when everyone walks out of the planning meeting isn't enough; writing down goals – whether they're personal goals or company objectives – requires discipline and increases the chances of effective implementation. Ultimately, the plan must answer the following questions: *What are we doing? Why? Who's doing it? By when? At what cost? For what expected result?* Studies show that people and companies with written goals consistently out-perform those without them. Writing requires focus. Focus drives effectiveness. Effectiveness increases performance. Write it down.

Take Action

You must enter the planning process with a commitment to implement the plan you and your team develop. A plan without action is a decision to do nothing. Lack of follow through wastes time, money and effort. More than that, failure to implement your plan after securing staff input is a cost to morale. Nothing saps a team's energy quicker than planning for an exciting future that will never be realized. So take action. People want to know *What will be different next week?* Make sure they know. Then show them with your actions. Remain disciplined as you move forward implementing the plan you developed. You can agree on exceptions to the timeline. Just follow through on your commitment to take action.

These five principles are the foundation to effective planning. If you want to get the most out of planning, make sure you and your team are committed to following them before you do anything else.

Take Action:

List the single biggest personal barrier that has the potential to hamper you and your team as you prepare to improve. Is it your impatience? A need to be right all the time? A lack of discipline to see things through to completion? Difficulty articulating what success looks like? Holding people accountable? Whatever it is, write it down in the space below. Confronting a shortcoming is the first step toward overcoming it.

_____

_____

_____

Now list three actions you'll take to address your issue and improve your personal effectiveness.

1. _____

2. _____

3. _____

"To achieve great things, two things are needed: A plan and not quite enough time."

~ Leonard Bernstein

5

Getting Ready to Plan

There are three phases to effective planning, and over the course of a year they will require a commitment of 73 hours of your time. That's not much time, but then you don't have much. Don't worry. Invested wisely, it's plenty.

The three phases are:

- Preparing for the planning session

- Conducting the planning session

- Implementing the plan & tracking accountability

Here's how you will invest your 73 hours over a 12-month period to increase your effectiveness and the effectiveness of those around you:

1 hour – Meeting to prepare for the planning session

16 hours – Participating in a two-day planning session

48 hours – Leading 24 twice-monthly two-hour account-ability meetings

8 hours   Participating in a day-long update session in another 4 – 8 months

_____

73 hours

There are 52 weeks in every year. Do the math and you'll see that each of the above activities occurs over a 51-week period. You're right. I've subtracted one week out of your year for a vacation. If you're not taking at least one week off every year because you believe the business can't operate well without you, there's a bigger problem to address in your operation. You'll be burned out (or worse) before you've reached your full potential. Planning will help you address this issue, too.

What You Need to Know

"Thought is action in rehearsal."

~ Sigmund Freud

What are the mechanics of organizing and conducting your company's planning process? Here's what you need to know to get ready for your initial two-day planning session.

When should you plan? The best time to plan is in the fourth quarter of your fiscal year. That's because your current year is complete enough to assess past performance (which is part of the process) before looking ahead and developing plans for the next fiscal year. Even if your business is seasonal, you've probably already got a pretty good idea of how you'll finish the year. Often, whether or not companies run their fiscal year on a January-December calendar, the period between Labor Day and Thanksgiving is another good time to hold your planning session. Perhaps it's the back-to-school mentality when summer vacations are behind us and company leaders return to more of a routine. I've facilitated planning sessions in the middle of summer, two weeks before Christmas and right after the first of the year. It can happen anytime. Don't confine your planning to a once- or twice-a-year event if there are pressing opportunities or challenges to address. When scheduling your planning session, select two back-to-back days that work best for you and your team, and give people enough notice so that they can clear their calendars. If some people must travel to attend the session, consider a Monday-Tuesday or Thursday-Friday schedule to minimize their time out of the office as well as time away from families. The main thing to keep in mind is that some times of the year are better for your business than other times, but anytime is better than not at all.

Who should lead the process? Hire an experienced facilitator to organize and lead your two-day planning process. You wouldn't perform surgery on yourself. Planning is like surgery without anesthesia. Why spend your limited time preparing to run the planning session when you can leverage your time and money hiring a pro to help you? Besides, it's unrealistic to expect you to run the meeting, watch meeting dynamics, think about and comment on issues, take notes and keep the meeting on topic and on time while keeping your personal biases in check. It simply can't be done. The baggage you carry is reason enough to have a third party lead the planning process. Everyone on the team may still try to give the answer they think you want to hear instead of speaking honestly, but a facilitator minimizes this tendency and will be viewed as a neutral resource with little, if any, baggage. Also, a facilitator carries no preconceived notions of what can or cannot be done by your organization. An outside perspective will help you and your team consider new ideas and reconsider old issues from fresh vantage points that you've previously taken for granted or dismissed. The facilitator's objective is producing a workable plan that improves your operations that all participants agree to implement. Look for a professional who's led planning sessions for companies your size or with your issues or both. When you think about the people from your company that you'll invite to the planning session – usually no fewer than three and sometimes as many as 20 – you'll conclude that a good facilitator will cost you less than the time of your executives who'll be giving up two days of working on the business. Why place their valuable time at risk? Ask your peers for resources they've used to help them plan. When you talk to the facilitator, ask for and then call their references. Once you've hired the facilitator, set a one-hour meeting to discuss exactly what you want to accomplish. A good facilitator that helps you develop a smart plan will return your investment in them 100-fold.

What do you want to accomplish? Your objective is to produce a written plan that will increase your company's performance and that everyone on your team will commit to implementing. (Check back in Chapter 3 to review the other results you should expect.) Invest the first hour of your 73 hours with the facilitator you've hired to agree on the specific outcomes you're expecting. What issues do you want to explore? Are there any topics that are off limits? There shouldn't be. Sacred cows, it's said, make the best hamburgers. Are there people who may be reluctant to speak whose opinions you really want to hear? Are there those who will dominate discussions if left unchecked? What tools, planning templates and exercises does the facilitator anticipate using? All of these issues and others specific to your business or industry should be discussed with the facilitator to prepare for a productive planning process.

Who should attend? Think carefully about who should attend the planning session. Most planning sessions can involve as few as three or as many as 20 leaders. The group size can grow, but 20 participants (with some exceptions such as planning for churches, schools, other not-for-profit organizations, government entities or Fortune 500 companies) should be the top end of your planning group. Everyone who reports directly to you should attend. All senior decision-makers with P&L responsibility. Partners, if that's how your organization is structured, should be there. What about board members and outside investors? You know their objectives and they should already be telling you what they think of your performance. Their participation at a planning session can be a distraction. Inform them of the outcomes of your planning session, but think twice about inviting them to participate. [If your organization is a not-for-profit entity, it's essential that board members be invited – and expected – to participate.] Are there people in your company whose industry or company knowledge makes their attendance worthwhile? Invite them. Many times, more than one sales person is included to obtain their perspective and to help them fully appreciate the issues faced by the rest of the organization. There may be others viewed as influential leaders even though their responsibility is limited. Consider the impact their participation in and commitment to the plan will have on the planning group and the company as a whole. Once you've determined who will attend, extend the invitation personally and help each invitee appreciate that their involvement in the planning process is an honor and privilege. Your choice of attendees determines what is discussed, what is decided and what will be done to help your company improve. If there are people in your organization whose feedback you want or who may be slightly offended at not being asked to attend the planning session, ask your facilitator to call these people in advance of the meeting to solicit their input. A sample memo to these non-participants plus sample questions are shown in the Appendix.

How much time should this take? Commit 16 of your 73 hours – two eight-hour days – to develop your written plan. There's certainly no one-size-fits-all approach to planning, however, the step-by-step approach we'll examine in Part 2 is an efficient, effective way for you and your top leaders to get the most out of your time together in two intense days. I should know. In the 25 years I've been involved in planning – as a participant, a CEO, and as a facilitator – I've seen a lot of time wasted on planning, and I know what's essential to developing an effective plan and what isn't. Get started at 8 or 8:30 a.m., work through lunch and call it a day around 5 or 5:30 p.m. If at the end of the day, you're on a roll and there's lots of energy around the discussion, keep going. Many times, leadership teams have dinner together after the first day of planning, and this can be productive on several levels. Start the second day at 8 or 8:30 a.m. and work until the plan is committed to paper. If there's been good discussion and good progress on the first day, you can typically wrap things up on the second day well before 5 p.m. You can take more than two days to plan, and occasionally it *is* necessary to allow more time for planning. [For not-for-profit groups whose leadership is comprised mostly of volunteers, it can be difficult to schedule back-to-back days for planning; additionally, the decision-making process in these organizations is much different from small and mid-sized companies, and takes much longer.] Most of the time, two days of planning is sufficient.

Where should you meet? Hold the meeting away from the office, if at all possible. Doing so eliminates workplace interruptions and helps participants stay focused on planning. A conference center or meeting room at a hotel is ideal. Request meeting rooms with no windows, good lighting and plenty of empty wall space to mount the notes from the flip charts you'll be writing down throughout the course of the two days. Make sure you can leave and lock the room after the first day because you'll have lots of paper covering the walls. If you're holding your session in a hotel meeting room that is adjacent to other meeting rooms, check out the acoustics and lighting controls beforehand. You'd don't want to be distracted by hearing your next door neighbors' session while you're trying to focus on yours, and you want to be sure that the two adjoining rooms have their own independent lighting controls and thermostats. I once conducted a session where the lights in our meeting began to dim as the group next door lowered the lighting to watch a video; we worked it out but it was a distraction. Resist the urge to hold your planning session in a hotel or country club room with a gorgeous view, otherwise people will spend their time gazing outside and wishing they were someplace else. The value of getting away to a neutral site sends a signal that this is not business as usual. If you select a hotel, you may decide it's worthwhile to ask every participant to spend the night there. Doing so makes scheduling dinner after the first day easy, and it also minimizes the likelihood of participants showing up late for the second day session. Refer to this meeting outside the office as a "planning session," "offsite," "strategic planning meeting" or some variation. Don't call it a "retreat." A retreat is moving backward. You want your plan to catapult you forward.

How should the room be arranged? Arrange tables in a U and position each of the two flips charts at each end of the U. This arrangement allows each participant to see one another and it allows the facilitator to enter the space to talk and work directly with each participant. For big groups, table tents with each person's name can be helpful. Don't worry about assigning seats to each participant. I watch the natural order of who sits where. Once the introductory portion of the day is completed, I re-arrange the seating to form new groups. Doing so helps balance personalities, politics and functional areas. It also sends a not-so-subtle signal that the next two days will be about making changes.

What materials and equipment will you need? You'll need a couple of flip charts on sturdy easels for notes, plus a set of permanent markers in multiple colors for writing. Bring tablets and pens for each participant. It's helpful for someone to bring their laptop, but most of the writing will be done on the flip charts. Talk with your facilitator about what other materials he or she needs. I keep a stack of 4x6-inch index cards handy and distribute these to participants and ask them to write their answer when anonymity is important or as part of anther exercise we're doing. Most facilitators will bring any other materials they plan to use. Sometimes, a TV with a DVD or Internet capability is helpful if there's a video it makes sense for the group to watch. You don't need a lot of equipment for a productive planning session – just the equipment between your ears.

What will your plan look like? My firm developed hundreds of plans for clients that took months to prepare and contained dozens of pages – sometimes as many as 200 pages. We were paid thousands of dollars and it sometimes seemed we were paid by the page. Unfortunately, if we weren't engaged beyond the planning phase to help with implementation, the full potential described in these plans rarely was achieved. Portions of the plan were executed, but never all of it. Why weren't these plans implemented as designed? One reason was that they were developed by us and not the people responsible for implementation. Another reason was that these planning documents were too long. Today, I favor more of a dashboard approach that whittles down a plan to your most significant objectives or priorities – usually no fewer than three and no more than seven. Based on these priorities, the planning team lists the actions that must be completed to achieve each objective. When finished, your plan will consist of between 10 and 20 pages. We'll cover this component thoroughly in Chapter 8, and I'll provide a planning template in the Appendix that you can use as a guide. Remember, less is more.

Will your team need to prepare anything? No. My view is that they've been preparing all their lives for this planning session. I don't make assignments before the meeting for two main reasons. First, most participants are so busy clearing two days on their calendar they won't take the time to do whatever it is they're asked to do before they sit down in the meeting. They may already feel burdened just attending; no need to add to this anxiety if it can be avoided. Second, I want everything that happens during the planning process to be the result of activities that occur in the room when everyone has the same opportunity to share the experience. There may be "homework" assignments given at the end of the first day, but advance preparation for the planning session is not necessary. Simply bring an open mind.

Will your team speak up? It depends on the group, but most people will speak up. We'll look at ways to create a safe place for people to say risky things in the guidelines section below. My experience is that most participants are eager to talk – even about uncomfortable issues. If you're not sure, ask the facilitator to prepare some questions to ask all participants on a confidential basis by phone or via email that can be completed and returned before the first planning session. The facilitator can then present this input at the meeting without attribution and encourage the group to discuss the issues. It's a question of trust and spontaneity versus security and thoughtful responses. It's the facilitator's job to get all the issues – good and bad – out in the open, discuss them, and, ultimately, gain agreement on whether the issues are priorities and, if so, how best to address them. Implicit disagreements cannot be ignored. Lack of alignment on significant issues will derail your plan before it has a chance to take off.

What guidelines should you follow? A planning session without open and honest discussion is a waste of time. If you can't talk about the real issues, don't expect your effectiveness, consistency and profitability to improve because you won't be addressing the things that are holding you back. Setting guidelines for the two-day planning sessions is critical. Every group should set their own during the first hour of the first day of planning. Write them down and keep them visible. Some companies have operating values that they transfer to the planning process. Whether you do or you don't, it's vital to ask the participants for the "rules" everyone will be following for their two days together. We'll look at eight fundamental rules in the next chapter.

Why have rules at all? Planning is a structured approach to opening your mind, unlocking creativity, and finding ways to improve effectiveness, consistency and profitability.

My wife Janet had the privilege of serving for many years as president of the Dallas office of DDB, one of the world's biggest and most respected advertising agencies. Creativity is their business. Remember the exploding mosquito for Tabasco brand pepper sauce? That's DDB.

But creativity is not confined to developing creative advertising. DDB is creative in their approach to planning and problem-solving, too. How does DDB encourage creativity? The agency developed "The Four Freedoms"...

Freedom from fear – Talent freezes in the grip of fear. The creative mind shuts down, constricting the natural flow of ideas. Fear is paralyzing beyond reason. It is not the truth that people fear. Fears results from not knowing the truth. Fear is created by motives that are suspect, by decisions made in secret for which the basis is not fully disclosed, and by the arbitrary use of power by those who control an idea's destiny. Fear is created by intimidation. Management by intimidation has no place in our organization.

Freedom to fail – It is the very nature of creative talent to venture beyond the known – to poke into the unheard of – to pick through scary places untrod by conventional minds. Because there are no assurances that such creative forays will succeed, the explorers must be granted freedom to fail in order to sustain their desire to venture forth again. It is the job of management to first point talented people in the right direction, then judge the value of their discoveries. But if the quest for the new is responsible and intelligent, talent must not be criticized for daring to fail.

Freedom from chaos – A degree of healthy ferment is required in any creative organization. But talent flounders in the chaos of uncertainty caused by management indecision, inconsistency, or vacillation. Talent requires benign discipline. The talented mind may seem erratic, but it welcomes an understanding of responsibilities that is clear, yet roomy enough to permit the floating dream. These responsibilities must be well understood and freely agreed to by all parties before an individual joins our organization. Once committed, all parties must live up to the agreement. It is particularly important that all management actions and communications be consistent with the understanding.

Freedom to be – The first priority of an organization that depends on its people for success must be the well-being of every individual. Each has a right to be treated with dignity, to be encouraged and supported in his or her ambitions for higher achievement, and, to the extent possible, to be provided with a place where a career can grow in the direction of the individual's own choosing. But beyond providing for professional growth, talented people must also be allowed to enjoy a life in which there is time for personal fulfillment, and for laughter and love and celebration.

Think about these freedoms in the context of your company's culture and how you conduct business, and then think about how they can help unlock creativity during your planning session.

You're now equipped with the benefits, principles and mechanics to gather your leaders to start planning.

Take action:

Make a list of possible planning dates and list the leaders you
plan to invite.

_____

_____

_____

_____

_____

_____

Part 2

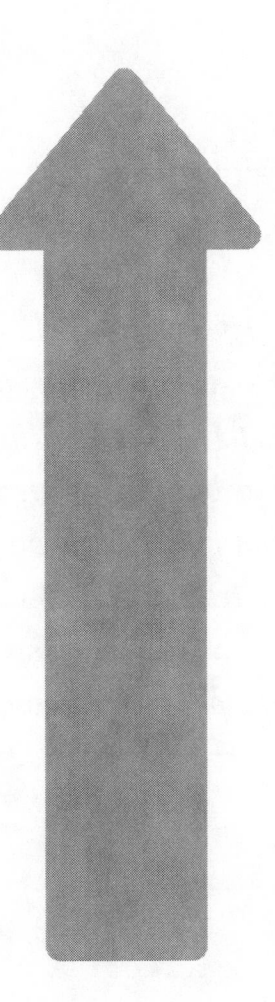

"Come to the edge," he said.
"No," they said, "we are afraid."
"Come to the edge," he said.
They came. He pushed them.
And they flew.

~ Guillaume Apollinaire

...Set...

"The basic paradox of freedom is that we are most free when we are bound. What matters is the character of our binding. The one who would be an athlete but who is unwilling to discipline his body…is not free to excel on the field or the track. His failure to train rigorously denies him the freedom to run with the desired speed and endurance. Discipline is the price of freedom."

~ Elton Trueblood

6

The First 90 Minutes of the First Day

The first 90 minutes of the first day and the last 30 minutes of the second day are the two most important blocks of time you and your team will spend together. Everything that happens in between during the next two days depends on these two hours.

The first 90 minutes sets the tone for:

- How each participant thinks, acts and contributes
- The degree to which issues are discussed candidly
- Individual and organizational improvement

The final 30 minutes of the second day is equally important because it determines whether the plan you and your team spent two days developing will be implemented and drive bottom-line improvement. More on the final half-hour in Chapter 9.

A sample agenda for the two-day planning session is shown in the Appendix.

Effective planning requires lots of thinking, and the best

thinking occurs when we structure issues so that our minds can see them clearly, and deal with them one facet at a time.

Structure unlocks creativity. Structure leverages time. Structure is how you get the right things done.

How you structure the planning process and how you move forward to address the ideas, questions and possibilities raised in your planning session will determine the degree to which your company can improve its effectiveness.

In 1999, after hundreds of engagements with the senior leaders of many of America's most admired large companies as well as with small and mid-sized businesses whose leaders we respected, my firm codified and patented a proprietary planning process called Quantum LEAPS®. It's certainly not a one-size-fits-all approach, but rather one that's customized for each organization's unique needs. Over the years we modified this process, adding exercises, questions, models and techniques while condensing the actual time spent on the process and, at the same time, increasing the participation of those who ultimately must implement the plan that's developed. Today, it's the best way I know of to help organizations increase their effectiveness.

You'll see in the diagram below that each exercise builds on the last one to result in your written plan:

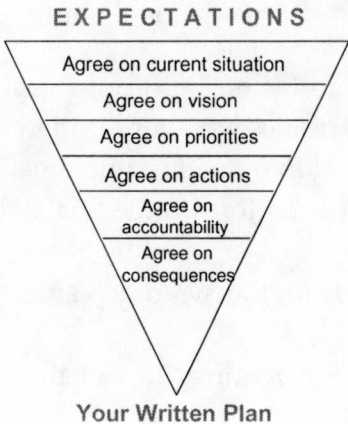

EXPECTATIONS

Agree on current situation

Agree on vision

Agree on priorities

Agree on actions

Agree on accountability

Agree on consequences

Your Written Plan

You won't find the "Take action" prompts at the end of each exercise that you've become accustomed to seeing throughout Part 1. Rather, each exercise in Part 2 generates one or more outcomes that will lead you and your team along a path toward developing your written plan. And that plan will become your roadmap to winning consistently.

The First Five Steps

"Coming together is a beginning. Staying together is progress. Working together is success."

~ Henry Ford

There are five exercises that you and your team should complete in the first 90 minutes of your planning session.

- Setting expectations

- Establishing clubhouse rules

- Assessing organizational performance

- Loosening Minds & Tongues

- Sharing Reflections & Celebrations

You may feel these exercises are being squeezed into a block of time that's too short to accommodate them. Not so. Executed properly, they can be completed effectively in 90 minutes.

What may dawn on you and every other participant during the next 90 minutes is the amount of time we're all capable of wasting each day. In the course of the next two days, you will see first-hand how a well-structured agenda increases productivity.

The brisk pace of the first 90 minutes generates a high level of energy and must be sustained during the entire planning session to keep attention focused, energy high, and creativity flowing.

Could a similarly focused approach to your business deliver the same high level of productivity? Absolutely.

Let's go.

Exercise #1

Setting expectations

"I am a great believer in luck and I find the harder I work, the more I have of it."

~ Thomas Jefferson

As the leader, it's your responsibility to re-confirm why this planning session is important, what you expect the planning process to accomplish and what you expect from each participant. I say "re-confirm" because you should have made these same points when you invited each participant to the offsite. [A sample invitation is shown in the Appendix.]

Prepare the three or four points of your opening remarks in advance. They should be short and to the point. Don't ramble.

Since one of your points will be describing the outcomes you expect (a written plan, leadership alignment and new opportunities for improving performance), you should mention that a key characteristic of an effective plan is that is consists of S.M.A.R.T. goals. What's the difference between a goal and an objective? Some people use these two words interchangeably. Here's the distinction I make. A goal is bigger, longer term, and should incorporate or reflect your company's mission and vision. An objective is the specific mile-marker along the way that lets you know you're making progress toward your goal. Both goals and objectives can and should be measured. [We'll cover this more fully in Part 3 when we examine implementing your plan.]

Go to the flip chart and write the word "Goals" at the top and "SMART" down the left-hand side of the flip chart, leaving room to write the word that corresponds to the letters in S.M.A.R.T.

Ask your team what each letter represents. Encourage responses from each participant but don't dawdle. Write down the correct words on the flip chart.

S Specific (i.e., clear and unambiguous)

M Measurable (i.e., quantifiably benchmarked)

A Attainable (i.e., realistic and achievable)

R Results-driven versus activity driven

T Time-based (i.e., there is a deadline)

Some participants may already know some or all of the words each letter represents. Others may not. Regardless, it's a quick way of showing your commitment to develop a plan together that will drive bottom-line results.

Tear off and post on the wall the "S.M.A.R.T. Goals" page.

It's important, too, that your team know what is *not* expected at this planning session.

This two-day planning session is neither an exercise in budgeting nor a substitute for good, sound budgeting. My belief is that there is no shortage of accounting software that can help with budgeting if this is something you've not had a lot of experience with. I also believe there's no shortage of people who are good with numbers – either inside your organization or outside it – that can calculate a set of numbers right down to the penny once you've figured out where you want to spend your money.

And that's the whole point of planning.

The budgets you and your team establish will be driven by determining your organization's biggest priorities and then allocating the necessary resources – time, money, talent – to achieve the desired outcomes associated with those priorities. Your budget should follow your priorities. Not the other way around.

Even with the "SMART" exercise your comments should take just five or six minutes. Once you've made your remarks, introduce the facilitator and take another minute to outline his or her credentials.

Note: I'm assuming you agree hiring a facilitator makes sense. A step-by-step guide will help you and your facilitator with your planning session. While each facilitator has his or her own way of running the meeting, I'm sharing the steps, exercises and questions that have been most effective in the hundreds of strategic planning meetings I've led and attended.

Exercise #2

Establishing Clubhouse Rules

*"Rules are for the obedience of fools and the
guidance of wise men."*

~ Sir Douglas Bader

We discussed operating guidelines in the last chapter, saying every group should adopt its own.

If you were ever part of a neighborhood or school club as a kid, you know that your club had rules. This is your planning club. It needs rules, too.

Your clubhouse rules make visible the expectations everyone should have of themselves and each other during the two days you're together.

Ask for suggestions about guidelines the entire group agrees to follow for getting the most out of the next two days. Why ask rather than post a list of rules? First, it keeps everyone thinking and participating. Second, the group will own and follow rules it makes for itself.

Start by asking *What rules or guidelines do we want to follow to make this planning session effective for each of us and the organization?*

Once the suggestions start coming, ask additional questions that can help steer the group toward articulating its own rules. Over the years, I've observed that seven fundamental guidelines must be in place to leverage your time investment and deliver the outcomes you expect from your planning meeting:

- All cell phones, PDAs and laptops are to be turned off

- Treat one another with respect

- Ask for and give honest feedback

- No side talking: If you've got something to say, say it to the group

- Silence equals agreement: Speak now or forever hold your peace

- Have fun

- Keep an open mind

These rules are self-descriptive, but I want to say a bit more about the importance of treating one another with respect and asking for and giving honest feedback. You won't get candor and honesty from the participants unless everyone knows and agrees to treat one another with respect. This means the participants believe the room is really safe to talk frankly about issues that range from the unusual to the controversial. Without getting these issues out in the open for a candid assessment of how they are affecting the organization, the planning session is diminished. Participants, as St. Paul once wrote, must be free to "speak the truth in love."

We'll examine the process of getting these issues out in the open in Chapter 6.

Write the group's thoughts on the flip chart underneath whatever title you like, say Clubhouse Rules.

Make sure each participant offers a suggestion, adds to one that's already been given or verbally seconds an existing suggestion.

This exercise should take about six or seven minutes.

Set a consequence – such as $1 donation to a newly established fund – for offenders, including the CEO. Agreeing on consequences, as we'll show later, is a critical component of driving execution and increasing effectiveness, and the symbolism of the $1 penalty raises awareness of the issue.

Once all input has been recorded, post the flip chart sheet in a prominent location where it will remain for the duration of the planning meeting. Encourage participants to call out one another whenever a rule is being stretched, broken, or ignored.

Exercise #3

Assessing Organizational Performance

"The success of each is dependent upon the success of the other."

~ John D. Rockefeller

Ask the group to take five minutes to complete the assessment you completed at the end of Chapter 1.

Once everyone has completed it, go around the room and ask them to give their scores. Write down all scores. Most always, there will be lots of good-natured comments as scores are given, usually variations of "Do we work for the same company?" and "You can tell he/she is an optimist/pessimist."

Highlight the lowest and highest scores.

Ask for people to read off the areas where scores are lowest and highest. Compare scores. Look for patterns.

Ask for feedback on the implications of these patterns. Ask the group what score the company should target six, nine or 12 months from now.

This is an opportunity to put into practice the principle of "Deciding how good you want to be." My experience has been that those companies genuinely interested in improving want to aim for excellence.

During this exercise, participants may raise issues that you and the group want to address. Now is probably not the time. Instead, write on the top of a flip chart page the words "Parking Lot" then write the issue or issues raised on this sheet. Tear off the page and ask for a volunteer to post it on the wall and to become the "Parking Lot Attendant." This person will be responsible during the first day for listening for issues that merit discussion and resolution but for whatever reason may not fit into the timeframe or exercise at the time the issue is first raised. Write the issue on the sheet with the expectation that it will be addressed before the planning session adjourns on the second day.

This entire exercise should take 20 to 30 minutes.

Exercise #4

Loosening Minds & Tongues

> *"A conclusion is the place where you got tired thinking."*
> ~ Martin H. Fischer

The group agreed to keep an open mind to possibilities and to have some fun.

Put both of these "rules" into action now with one of these three exercises. Or choose one of your own.

Exercises like this limber up the minds around the table and keep everyone involved. We'll do lots of exercises throughout the day, and there are plenty included in this book for you to choose from.

Regardless of which of the three exercises you choose, ask everyone to take 60 seconds to prepare their answers on an index card. Take another five or six minutes to go around the room and ask each participant for their solution.

Diamond & Water

Ask participants to write down on their card which of these two items they consider more valuable: a diamond or a bucket of water.

Both answers can be correct. The ultimate answer is: "It depends." It's easy to say that a diamond is the more valuable of the two – unless, of course, you're in a desert where a bucket of water can save your life.

The lesson: An idea that may at first glance appear to be almost worthless could become a valuable solution when it is placed in a new surrounding or viewed from a different vantage point.

Rabbit & Duck

Show the participants the image below.

Ask them to write down what they see.

You may be interested to know that this exercise is credited to American psychologist Joseph Jastrow (1863 – 1944) who based his drawing on one that originally appeared in *Harper's Weekly* in 1892, which in turn is based on a drawing that appeared earlier that same year in *Fliegende Blätter*, a German humor magazine. Jastrow used the drawing to show how a single image can offer the eye two competing perspectives. He noted that our views are shaped by our life experiences.

Whether you see a duck or a rabbit, you are correct.

The lesson: There can be more than one correct answer to a problem. Look at issues from multiple perspectives to find the best solution.

Stick Man & Wood

On the flip chart, draw a stick figure of a person holding a piece of wood in their hand.

Ask each participant to draw the same thing on an index card, and then draw the position of the wood when it's released.

After 60 seconds, ask each participant to walk to the flip chart and draw on the chart what they drew on their index card. Ask the first participant to hand the marker to a participant of their choice until all participants have drawn their answer.

You will likely get similar versions from all participants. Don't worry – this will simply reinforce your point.

When all participants have provided their answers, congratulate them on being correct.

Most all participants will have assumed that the stick person was standing on land, so the block of wood drops to the ground.

There are variations on the answer, ranging from the wood

bounced, splintered, broke into pieces, hit my shin then fell to the ground. But invariably, most if not all participants will make the assumption that the man is standing on land, and gravity has done its thing.

But what if the stick person were standing in water up to his neck?

The wood floats to the top.

What if the stick person were in space?

The wood remains stationary.

The lesson: Don't assume you already know the answer. Look at a situation from more than one perspective, and you will likely come up with more than one correct answer.

[See the Appendix for two more quick exercises that demonstrate the speed with which humans lock in on solutions, answers and beliefs. The exercises are Mental Traits to Consider and The Power of an Open Mind.]

At this point, you should have about 40 minutes left to complete the next exercise.

Exercise #5

Reflections & Celebrations

> *"In Italy for 30 years under the Borgias, they had warfare, terror, murder, bloodshed. They produced Michelangelo, Leonardo da Vinci and the Renaissance. In Switzerland, they had brotherly love, 500 years of democracy and peace, and what did they produce? The cuckoo clock."*
>
> ~ Orson Welles

This exercise focuses on each individual.

Ask each participant to take five minutes to answer these three questions on an index card:

- What three things are you most proud of having accomplished in the last 12 months? (these can include personal accomplishments as well as business achievements)

- What is your single biggest disappointment of the last 12 months?

- What do you want to celebrate 12 months from now (or at the end of this year, or at the end of next year)?

After five minutes, ask each participant to share what he or she wrote. Consider asking one of the more reticent participants to volunteer to speak first. Make sure the senior-most executives speak last, with the CEO the very last to speak. If the CEO speaks first, there may be a tendency for all other comments to reflect the CEO's views.

Determine the amount of time each participant can speak based on the size of the group.

As each participant says what he or she wrote, post all responses on three separate sheets – one each for Accomplishments, Disappointments and Celebrations – and write their names by each comment.

This exercise works on several levels:

- It forces each person to be honest with themselves and one another
- It demonstrates the pledge of making the environment a safe place for candor
- It allows all participants to see what their peers consider significant
- It sets a benchmark for determining what's working and not working in people's lives and in the organization
- It helps gauge the extent to which everyone is or is not on the same page
- Thinking about a "celebration" instead of "objectives" helps people think differently about what they consider "success"
- It provides a logical jumping off point to probe for improvement

Wrap up the first 90 minutes by gaining agreement from the entire group on what everyone will be celebrating as a company 12 months from now (or whatever comparable time period you want to set).

You may reach consensus easily.

Oftentimes, however, this question sparks spirited discussion and occasionally even some healthy disagreement about the celebration. This response is not unusual, especially as the leadership team reconciles the findings from the organizational assessment with its hopes for the company's future.

A little passion this early in the day is a good sign that you're off to a productive planning session. You can't celebrate a victory without a few battles.

Continue working to gain consensus. This is important. You've just set the direction for the rest of your two-day planning session – and your company's future.

Turn the page (or take a 10-minute break) and get set for some small-group problem-solving.

"It is not enough just to do your best and work hard. You must know what to work on."

~ W. Edwards Deming

7

The Rest of the First Day

We began the day asking questions, and the rest of the first day consists of asking many more increasingly pointed questions.

The power of questions is undisputed.

Depending upon your point of view, however, asking questions can be painful or pleasant. Some participants – even those at the very top of the organization – may feel that placing certain questions before the group forces them to confront important issues they would rather not discuss or perhaps even think about. Other participants may find the process of asking questions liberating because an issue that inhibits the organization's effectiveness is now open for discussion among the leadership team.

Either way, asking and answering these questions is essential, and the planning process offers the ideal time and safe environment to address these important issues. (Remember your clubhouse rules about honesty and respect.)

You know the issues I'm talking about, right? These issues are the proverbial elephants in the room. Everyone knows that these big guys are there, and everyone does their best to stay out of their way. There typically is a handful of significant issues that are so big that everyone on the leadership team knows

69

they're there, but for whatever reason – fear of retribution, potential embarrassment at being the one to speak the unspeakable, lack of confidence in believing a particular issues really is significant, hope that the issue will resolve itself, etc. – the issue is carefully avoided.

Where is the company headed? Why has our growth stalled? Why are our profits shrinking? Why is morale so bad? Why are we losing our best customers? Everyone knows the laggards who are holding us back – why can't we fire them?

Not all questions, of course, are controversial or troubling.

But asking questions so that each person on the entire leadership team can weigh in with his or her perspective ensures that everyone's on the same page by the time your two-day planning session is completed.

We've already said that asking questions exposes blind spots, illuminates possibilities and provides focus and clarity.

Answering questions helps organizations isolate important issues and set priorities. Answers confirm the values, beliefs and activities that are working well and provide focus on areas that must be improved. This process helps achieve alignment among the leadership team. Armed with this more refined understanding makes you more effective in the activities you choose to undertake.

Here are five more exercises that will move your organization another step closer to higher levels of effectiveness and profitability. Let's examine each of them in order.

Exercise #6

What Is and Isn't Working?

"The trouble with most of us is that we would rather be ruined by praise than saved by criticism."
~ Norman Vincent Peale

Let's examine the story behind the scores from the assessment in today's opening minutes.

Divide the group into small groups so there are at least three people in each group.

Ask those in each group to raise their right hand then point it at someone else in their group. The person with the most votes in each group becomes the leader.

Go to the flip chart and write these three sets of questions:

1. What's working? Why?

2. What's not? Why?

3. What is our profit? What should it be?

Explain that each group will answer these questions in 20 minutes and report back to the entire group. This is plenty of time because we're simply confirming information that's top of mind with everyone in the room, but this exercise gives us an opportunity to see the extent to which leaders are already aligned on these issues.

If some or all of the participants have not been exposed to a profit figure, that's okay. If this is the case, this issue in and of itself is a telling indicator. Shouldn't all of your leaders know what your profit is and should be? If they don't, how are they going to be focused on helping improve it? Even if people don't know what the profit target is, ask them to reach their best conclusion. Whether the figure they share with the larger group is on the money, in the ballpark or totally off the mark provides another discussion point.

Once the small groups are assembled, the leader makes sure everyone on his or her team provides input on the questions, and that all questions are answered in the allotted time. The leader can select a spokesperson and/or a note taker (sometimes it's the same person). As the CEO, you should not be a permanent part of any group, but can visit with each group to see how they're doing and to answer any questions they may have. [Depending upon how your company is structured, with multiple partners or a COO, you can make the call about who is in whose group. The idea is to see what conclusions your direct reports and other leaders reach.]

After 20 minutes, bring the small groups back together.

Ask each leader to report his or her group's conclusions, with the note-taker recording the answers on a flip chart. Do this with each group. Keep it moving.

When all answers have been shared and posted, ask the group to look for areas of commonality. There are usually several strong points for the company that each group has listed. Circle these. Likewise, there are usually several problem areas that each group has listed. Circle these.

After hearing each small group present their conclusions, ask if there are other strengths or problem areas your group omitted that should have made your list. Write down any new input. This portion of the exercise should take another 20 or 25 minutes.

Tear off the flip chart pages, post them on the wall, and tell the group that we will come back to these later today.

The entire exercise should take between 40 and 45 minutes.

Exercise #7

Who Are You?

"Be yourself – everyone else is already taken."
~ Oscar Wilde

You've got to know yourself before you can be yourself.

Use the model below – which I call an Identity Pyramid – to articulate your history, define points of difference and confirm what's most important to you as well as to those you serve.

Keep the entire planning group together that previously re-assembled to share their conclusions of what's working and what isn't working.

Draw a triangle on a flip chart and label the sections as shown below:

Move to the second flip chart and draw another triangle,

dividing the triangle into seven sections but leaving the sections blank.

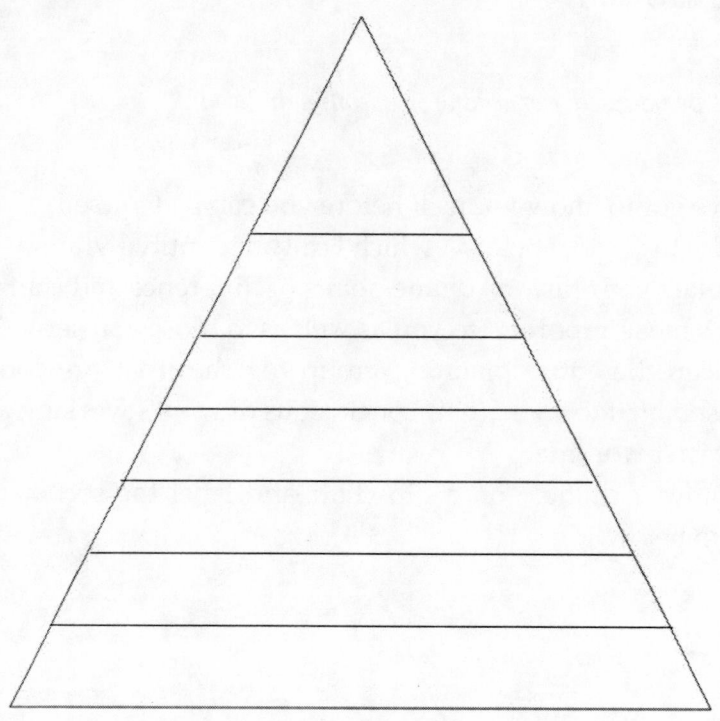

Start at the bottom – your foundation – and ask for input on the first level: "History & Values." Write down all comments. You can edit them later to a few words or phrases that represent the most significant events that have defined and shaped your organization.

Allow 7 to 12 minutes per section.

As the leader, you've probably got a pretty clear idea about how you'd complete each section. What may surprise you as you move forward with this exercise is the difference of opinion that emerges from your leadership team, especially as you and your team work your way up the triangle.

The first three sections of the triangle are your organization's foundation, and reflect where you've been and who you are today. These sections should be completed relatively easily.

As you move toward the top of the triangle, your perspective should gradually shift from a historical perspective to a current perspective and, ultimately, to a future state. The going will get a little tougher and slower as everyone takes a crack at providing their take on each section. Keep things focused and moving.

As you begin to complete the model, you will find that you are asking and answering other related questions, such as these:

- *How would we describe our company today? What is our culture?*

- *How would our customers and prospects describe our company?*

- *What is our unfair advantage that causes our customers to select us over our competition?*

- *Where will future profitable growth come from?*

- *What is it about our best customers that we appreciate the most?*

Your answers for the top section – "Your ideal customer" – may include traits from a single customer or client, or may represent a composite picture of the traits of some of your best customers. It's up to you and your team to define what you mean by "best."

Over the years, my firm developed a list of 100 Critical Questions we used in planning sessions with our clients. This list of questions along with two other exercises – The Positioning Portrait™ and the Value Revelation Chain™ – are shown in the Appendix.

As one part of this exercise, be sure to devote some time to listing your Strengths, Weaknesses, Opportunities and Threats, or SWOTs. Write each word on a separate flip chart page and ask for input for each of these four areas. This portion of the exercise is a natural addition to the work you are doing to sharply define who you are as an organization, and this input will be necessary when it comes time on the second day to establish your organizational priorities.

It's important to achieve consensus on each section of the triangle because this exercise becomes another layer in your planning foundation as you move toward increasing your organization's overall effectiveness.

This exercise should take 90 minutes.

Exercise #8

What Is Your Competitive Advantage?

"The buyer rarely buys what the seller thinks he's selling."

~ Peter Drucker

Why do people buy from you instead of someone else?

If you can't articulate a compelling reason succinctly, don't expect your customers and prospective customers to be able to do so either.

That's why it's critical for an organization to find its intrinsic competitive advantage and then leverage it. By "intrinsic" I mean that your competitive advantage most likely already exists within your company. It's the essence of your company.

The key is to make certain you are capitalizing on this advantage to the full extent possible. *Have you made your competitive advantage a centerpiece with your stakeholders? Are you charging what you should based on the value this advantage offers your customers? Have you articulated your advantage in a way that is easily understood and compelling?*

If your answer to any of these three questions is "no" or "I'm not sure," this next exercise will help.

There's a little bit of chicken-and-egg logic that goes on here. Which comes first? Defining your vision or articulating your competitive advantage?

I believe you must first confirm what it is that your company does best – that's a cornerstone of your competitive advantage – and then you build upon this strength. You and your team already worked through some of this in the previous exercise.

This next exercise focuses solely on reducing your competitive advantage to a short, compelling statement. The exercise is predicated on the assumption that your company is already

reasonably successful and that you're using the planning process to increase your effectiveness and profitability.

Unless you're completely overhauling your company, and
staking a new vision that is significantly different from your
current course, I recommend moving forward in the order I've
presented here.

Divide your large group back into groups of three or four
persons each. Change the make-up of each of the small groups
from what it was in the earlier small groups so that a new mix
of people is assembled. Doing this keeps the energy level high,
injects new personalities and perspectives into the mix and
provides the opportunity for everyone to interact with one another at a small-group level.

Each group is given 45 minutes to answer the following
question:

> *How can our company create and occupy a "position" in the mind
> of those we serve and want to serve that reflects our strengths and
> weaknesses as well as those of our competitors?*

Here are five steps each group should take to help them
draw some initial conclusions about your company's competitive advantage.

1. Ask the group to review the list of the company's strengths.
    Ask the group to place a check mark alongside any strengths
    that are unique to the company – a product or service that
    no other company provides in any form whatsoever. If you
    see that you do indeed have strengths that are unique to the
    company, you must ask if you are conveying those strengths
    in a compelling manner. If they are not unique to you, new
    ones must be uncovered or developed and communicated.

2. Tell the group that successful companies understand what
    their customers consider most valuable, whether that value
    is translated as time, price, quality, peace of mind, service

or some other benefit. Michael Treacy and Fred Wiersema identified "three distinct value disciplines" which they expressed as operational excellence, innovation and "customer intimacy," or customization and service. Exceptional companies are proficient to some degree in all three of these areas, but they choose one of the three disciplines to "master" and then they stake their market reputation on that discipline. For operational excellence, think Southwest Airlines and Wal-Mart. For innovation, think Apple Computer and 3M. For customization, think Nordstrom's and the brokerage firm A.G. Edwards. Ask each group to determine which of these three traits best describes your organization and ask them to explain why.

3. Tell the group that a reward or benefit must be at the heart of your position. This reward or benefit resides in the mind of those you serve and seek to serve – it does not reside in your product or service. In other words, a product attribute is not a reward. Direct them to answer these three questions: *What do we do better than anyone else? Why do our customers consider this product or service we provide to be better than that which our competitors provide? If we charged more for this product or service, would our customers still buy from us?*

Walk around to monitor each group's progress. After each group has answered the questions listed above, give them their fourth assignment.

4. Instruct the group to look at the answers to each of the three questions and to go back and ask "Why?" five times for each of the three answers they've developed. This method, first developed by Sakichi Toyoda and later employed by the Toyota Motor Company, is called, not surprisingly, The Five Why's. Its name derives from the practice of asking, five times, why a failure has occurred or a belief is held in

order to drill down to the root cause or causes of a problem, opportunity or issue. Here's an example:

- My car will not start. (the problem)

- *Why?* The battery is dead. (First why)

- *Why?* The alternator is not functioning. (Second why)

- *Why?* The alternator has broken beyond repair. (Third why)

- *Why?* The alternator is well beyond its useful service life and has never been replaced. (Fourth why)

- *Why?* I have not been maintaining my car according to the recommended service schedule. (Fifth why, root cause)

This method is not fool-proof and there are limitations to its effectiveness, yet it is a quick way to force people to look beyond symptoms or easy answers and drill down to systemic causes.

5. Once each group has completed these steps, give them the formula below and ask them to fill in the blanks.

_____ **is the brand of** _____

for _____ **that** _____

because _____.

Study these three examples to help you develop your company's position:

**McDonald's is the brand of restaurant
for families that want good, fast,
inexpensive meals because McDonald's
serves me quickly and has something that
everyone will love.**

Southwest Airlines is the brand of **airline**
for **business travelers** that **want low fares,
low frills and on-time flights** because **Southwest
has the lowest fares and the best on-time performance
record in the airline industry.**

Dial is the brand of **deodorant soap**
for **people that want to feel fresh, clean and
confident** because **Dial has twice as much
deodorant ingredients as the next best
selling brand.**

This devilish little tool will help you clarify your company's "positioning." You'll soon discover how devilishly maddening it is as you reduce into two dozen well-chosen words what your company stands for or does best. The idea of "positioning" was developed by Al Ries and Jack Trout in 1981 as a way to think about the position your company, product or service occupies in the mind of a customer or prospect. This formula can be the key to unlocking your competitive advantage. Complete this exercise to find, confirm or modify your position in the marketplace that you can stake out, own and defend.

As you think about positioning – or repositioning – your organization, product or service, be sure to apply these four critical tests:

1. Your position must reflect values you hold dear

2. Your position must be clearly understood in your prospect's mind

3. Your position must be singular – you cannot be all things to all people

4. Your position must set you apart – it must be distinctive and compelling

What's critical to remember is that if your brand's promise is not supported by performance, promotional efforts actually erode your brand's value. For that reason, employees are a crucial link to your other constituents. When employees understand and reflect the core brand values, they radiate out to customers and other stakeholders.

In the case of virtually all successful companies, performance more than matches the promotion. A brand is really a promise. So be sure your brand can keep the promise it makes to your stakeholders.

Once each group has completed these five steps, bring them back together and ask them to share the entire group their conclusions from Step 2 and Step 5.

Ask each group to write their conclusions on a flip chart page.

When all groups have provided their input, begin the process of gaining consensus. It's not uncommon for groups to have different points of view on the conclusions from Step 2. Make the advocates of opposing points of view explain their position to the entire group. Let them persuade others on the team to the position they are advocating. Use common sense. If the group is evenly divided, you as the chief executive must make the call.

Repeat the process of building consensus for Step 5. Remember, this phrase is not necessarily going to appear on a T-shirt or company coffee mug (although sometimes they do). So don't worry if the language is a little clumsy or the words don't exactly trip off your tongue. The important thing to keep in mind is that this phrase will become the lens through which your vision, priorities and future initiatives are viewed. [For a visual depiction of the importance of positioning, refer to the Positioning Waterfall in the Appendix.]

Once the small groups have been re-assembled to present their conclusions, the consensus-building activity may take 45 minutes to an hour to complete.

This is heavy lifting. Keep things moving, but give the discussion time and don't get frustrated if things seem to bog down a little. This exercise is one of the most significant ones in the entire two days because it is helping you bring laser-like focus to your business.

The entire exercise should take 90 minutes to up to two hours.

At this point the end of the first day is right around the corner. There's just one more exercise before we call it a day.

Exercise #9

Where Are You Going?

"Vision without action is a daydream. Action without vision is a nightmare."

~ Japanese proverb

As CEO, you've probably got a pretty clear idea of what you're trying to accomplish with your business.

Unfortunately, my experience has shown that in most cases, few other people in the company know precisely what that is.

Your employees know at a pretty basic level what's supposed to be happening. Everyone wants the company to succeed. And everyone wants to keep their job and make more money.

That's not what I'm talking about. I'm talking about a specific, crystal clear vision that's simple to understand and has an element of inspiration to it.

Your vision should be a short, succinct, and inspiring statement of what the organization intends to become and to achieve at some point in the future, often stated in competitive terms. It should be broad and forward-thinking. It is the image that an organization must have of its goals before it sets out to reach them. It describes aspirations for the future, without specifying the means that will be used to achieve those desired ends.

News flash: A financial objective is *not* a vision.

While the vision statement can be developed during the planning session, the vision itself must be set by the chief executive or senior-most person in the organization. The success of an enterprise depends on it.

Don't confuse a mission with a vision.

A mission is the organization's purpose. What the organization is about. It's your passion. You confirmed your mission two exercises ago with the Identity Pyramid.

A vision is where the organization is trying to go.

And strategy is the roadmap for getting you there.

Consider these mission and vision statements from three highly respected companies:

Southwest Airlines

Mission: "Dedication to the highest quality of Customer Service delivered with a sense of warmth, friendliness, individual pride, and Company Spirit."

Vision: "The Freedom to Fly." (e.g., providing affordable air travel for all Americans…not just a few.)

The Container Store

Mission: "To provide innovative products and a high level of customer service in order to help people get organized, save space, and ultimately, save time."

Vision: "To be the destination of choice for people who need help organizing any area of their home or office."

Microsoft Corporation

Mission: "At Microsoft, we work to help people and businesses throughout the world to realize their full potential. This is our mission. Everything we do reflects our mission and the values to make it possible."

Vision: "A computer for every person."

As previously noted, I'm assuming that as the CEO you have a pretty clear idea of what you want to accomplish and where you want to lead your company. [If your vision isn't somewhat defined, work with your facilitator before the group planning session begins to put into words your thoughts on where you see the company going.]

At this point in the planning session, your facilitator will acknowledge that all of these exercises are building on one another, and that it's now time to hear from you with your thoughts on where you want this company to go. Aristotle said, "The soul never thinks without a picture." It's time to give your leadership team your picture of the future. Your vision should be more far-reaching than the one-year celebrations that have already been agreed to earlier in the day.

Take a few minutes to outline in broad strokes or in some specific terms where you see the company in three, five or even 10 years. Your remarks are not so much about giving a rah-rah speech as they are about helping everyone on the leadership team understand what's important to you and what your long term dreams are for the company, your customers and your colleagues. Your remarks don't need to be polished, but they need to convey clearly the direction you see for the organization.

This should only take about five minutes and certainly no more than 10.

Once you've concluded your remarks, invite questions and ask for feedback. Once questions have been answered and positions clarified, it's the group's turn to help turn your vision into a compelling statement.

A vision must be conveyed in a dramatic and enduring way for it to have any lasting impact on your stakeholders. The most effective visions are those that inspire, usually asking stakeholders (most often employees but also investors and those outside the organization that you seek to serve) for the best, the most, the first or the greatest. Warren Bennis, the pioneer of contemporary leadership studies and advisor to four U.S. presidents, said "A powerful enough vision can transform what would otherwise be loss and drudgery into sacrifice."

Once again, divide your large group into smaller groups and ask each group to develop a vision statement for the company based on your remarks. Instruct each group to write their proposed vision statement on a sheet from the flip chart. As the CEO, you should not assign yourself to a group, but circulate among the groups to answer questions, pose a question or two of your own and monitor progress.

This portion of the exercise should take about 20 minutes.

Bring everyone back together and ask each group to present their proposed vision statement. Each group should write on the flip chart the vision statement they've developed.

After each group has presented, gain consensus on a vision statement for the company. Write it down.

At this point in the day, every participant should be feeling physically and emotionally spent. And with good reason. A lot of very important work has been completed and the stage is now set for a productive day tomorrow.

My experience is that some CEOs tend to minimize the work done by the teams on this first day. CEOs believe everyone should already know this information. CEOs are ready to solve problems and prepare the written plan.

Remember that planning is equal parts emotion and intellect. By going through this process, the emotional aspects of buy-in are beginning to occur. It's hard work and most people are tired – mentally and physically.

In addition to feeling drained, every single leadership team that I've worked with as a planning facilitator is genuinely excited when they reach this point. Most groups actually applaud themselves or high-five one another once a vision statement has been developed.

That's one indicator that you've got a vision that's big, bold and inspiring.

And it's the perfect place to call it day.

There's just one more quick thing you need to do before you adjourn.

Exercise #10

One More Thing...

"Feedback is the breakfast of champions."
~ Ken Blanchard

Before adjourning, go to the flip chart and draw a vertical line down the center of the page to create two columns.

On one side at the top of the left-hand column, write "Strengths" or a plus sign (**+**). On the right-hand column, write "Changes" or a delta sign (**Δ**), the Greek letter used by scientists and mathematicians to symbolize change.

Starting on the "strengths" side, ask your team what they liked about the day. Summarize their answers with a word or two or a short phrase and write their responses on the flip chart. You may experience some silence at first, so give everyone time to speak up and offer their thoughts. There should be at least a half-dozen things about the day that they valued.

Don't debate, critique or comment on the responses. Just make sure that everyone understands the meaning behind the remarks.

Next, ask them what they would change about the day. Again, summarize and record their responses on the "changes" side of the flip chart.

Both sets of feedback are important because it helps everyone understand what's already been accomplished in a single day, while providing suggestions and insights on ways to address distractions and improve the planning process on the second day of planning.

This exercise should take about five or six minutes.

You've now concluded the business portion of the day.

My experience has been that some social time for the entire group makes a lot of sense at this point in the planning process. The social time is a miniature celebration for a productive day.

It provides an excellent opportunity for people who may not work together much or see one another very often to interact in a casual setting. And it's a great jumping off point before re-convening the next morning.

You can decide what makes sense for your organization – a 90-minute happy hour or, ideally, a group dinner. Whatever you decide, enjoy you time together but don't overdo it. You'll be right back at it early the next morning.

"Always bear in mind that your own resolution to succeed is more important than any one thing."

~ Abraham Lincoln

8

The Second Day

The second day of your two-day planning session is when you and your team will commit your plan to writing and commit to each other to implement the plan you develop. You will literally begin to chart the course you will take to winning on a consistent basis.

Start the second day by quickly reviewing what you and your team accomplished yesterday. It's a good idea to write these eight accomplishments on a flip chart. You have gained agreement on:

- Understanding what S.M.A.R.T. goals are and their importance in planning
- Setting (and, I trust) abiding by your clubhouse rules
- Establishing a baseline indicator of the company's current performance with the assessment
- Establishing celebrations for the future
- Establishing what is and isn't working and what your profit is and should be
- Defining who you are as an organization
- Defining and articulating your competitive advantage

• Defining your vision

These eight items are significant accomplishments. You and your team should be proud of the work you've completed.

Yesterday was all about possibilities. Today is all about getting results.

Without a written plan and a commitment from all participants to execute it, the work you did yesterday will have been wasted. You're not going to let that happen, are you?

Turn the page to take the next step to begin charting your course to win.

Exercise #1

Jump Starting the Second Day

"If you start to take Vienna, take Vienna."
~ Napoleon Bonaparte

Yesterday morning, one of the first exercises undertaken was asking all participants to solve a riddle.

You'll recall the purpose of that exercise was to "loosen tongues and minds."

After reviewing yesterday's accomplishments, ask each participant to take an index card and write their answer to each of these two questions – one answer on one side, another answer on the back of the card.

Here's the first question:

What one thing – if you started doing it consistently – would improve your effectiveness?

Now the second question:

What one thing – if you stopped doing it – would improve your effectiveness?

Give everyone two to three minutes to complete their responses. Ask them to set down their pens or pencils when they're through.

Before asking everyone to share their answers, ask all participants to number off 1-2, 1-2, 1-2 until all participants have been paired with someone. [I usually tell the CEO that he or she will be paired with me.]

This pairing represents each person's accountability partner. More than just a way to jump-start the day, specific areas for improvements are being identified and commitments are being made.

Before asking each participant to read their responses, ask yesterday's Parking Lot Attendant to name a new person to handle the Parking Lot duties for the day.

As each participant gets ready to read their responses, instruct each accountability partner to:

- Listen carefully to what his or her partner is saying

- Take notes listing the action your partner is committing to take

- Make sure the actions are clear and specific

- Think about how you – as the accountability partner – can support your partner's commitment

Now go around the room and have each person read their responses.

In some planning sessions I've facilitated, the CEO has asked the team for feedback on his or her performance. Tell me, the CEO says, your response to *What should I start doing?* and *What should I stop doing?*

A CEO that asks for this feedback raises the ante and demonstrates a powerful approach to leadership.

Time Management Tips

We've said all along that effective time management can be a difficult matter for even the most efficient leaders.

Just remember: Time is not the enemy. Wasting time is. Because lost time can never be recovered.

Focus and discipline drive productivity and effectiveness. And focus and discipline are the keys to time management.

At some point in the Start-Stop exercise, quickly share these time management approaches from three of the most successful business leaders of all time who know the importance of committing goals to paper and the value of careful time management.

Stephen Covey uses a four-box quadrant in which he places activities that are urgent but not important, urgent and important, not urgent and not important, and not urgent but important.

Covey's View of Time Management

	urgent	not urgent
Important	Activities Crises Pressing problems Deadline-driven projects	Activities Prevention Relationship-building Recognizing new opportunities Planning Recreation
Not Important	Activities Interruptions, some calls Some mail, some reports Some meetings Near, pressing matters Popular activities	Activities Trivia, busy work Some mail and email some phone calls Time wasters Pleasant activities

Southwest Airlines Chairman Herb Kelleher makes two columns – one that reads, "Must be completed today" and the other that reads, "Can be completed tomorrow."

Herb Kelleher's View of Time Management

Must be completed today	**Can be completed tomorrow/ next week**
Activities	Activities
1. _____	1. _____
2. _____	2. _____
3. _____	3. _____
4. _____	4. _____
5. _____	5. _____
6. _____	6. _____
7. _____	7. _____
8. _____	8. _____

There's an even simpler approach, and it's the one I favor.

About 100 years ago, management consultant Ivy Lee called on Charles M. Schwab, president of Bethlehem Steel and a protégé of Andrew Carnegie.

Schwab was a typically impatient chief executive and reportedly said to Lee that he "wanted less knowing and more doing" in his company.

Lee responded by handing Schwab a blank piece of paper and asking him to list all of the important tasks he wanted to complete. After Schwab completed the list, Lee told him to number each task in order of importance. After Schwab completed this assignment, Lee advised Schwab to place the paper in his pocket then take it out the following morning and work on that item until it was completed. Once item one was completed, Lee told Schwab he was to tackle item two in the same way, then item three and so on. "Do this until quitting time each day," Lee said. "Don't be concerned if you only complete one or two items each day. The other items can wait, and you will be working on the most important items. When you complete the list, make and number a new list."

Lee, the story goes, said, "If you can't finish your tasks with this method, then you probably couldn't finish them with any other method. And without this system, you couldn't even decide which items are most important."

Lee concluded the meeting by telling Schwab to "send me a check for what you think this advice is worth." Some weeks later, Schwab sent Lee a check for $25,000 – at a time when a day's wages were $2.

The lesson: Staying focused on completing one task at a time is an extremely effective way to accomplish your most important tasks

Ivy Lee's View of Time Management

List all activities. Circle the six you must complete today.

Activities

1. _____

2. _____

3. _____

4. _____

5. _____

6. _____

7. _____

8. _____

9. _____

10._____

11._____

12._____

13._____

14._____

15._____

Look simple? Try it.

Decide right now which of these three time management

systems is right for you. If you have another system that's already working for you, that's fine. Ask each participant about their personal time management system. If they don't have one, ask them which system they're going to adopt. If they already have a system but haven't been using it, ask them to re-commit themselves to a system that will increase their effectiveness and the effectiveness of the work area that they oversee.

This exercise should take 30 minutes to an hour to complete, depending on the number of participants and the amount of feedback the CEO receives.

While adopting or modifying one of these three time management techniques to set and achieve personal priorities, you'll need another approach for identifying, agreeing to and implementing organizational priorities.

Let's address that topic with the next exercise.

Exercise #2

What's Most Important?

"Decide what you want, decide what you are willing to exchange for it. Establish your priorities and go to work."
~ H.L. Hunt

It's one thing to establish your own priorities but quite another to establish priorities for an entire organization.

One reason is because there are lots of important things that need to get done in your business. How do you and your leaders decide which ones are most important?

Divide the large group once again into several smaller groups with at least four participants per small group.

Before sending them off on their next assignment, ask for a volunteer to read from the flip charts that you posted yesterday about what is and isn't working, your triangle that defines who you are, and your four sheets with your SWOTs.

Once that's been done, tell them about the mayonnaise jar and beer.

Mayonnaise Jar & Beer

A professor stood before his philosophy class with several items in front of him.

When the class began, wordlessly, he picked up a large and empty mayonnaise jar and began filling it with golf ball-sized rocks. He then asked the students if the jar was full. They agreed that it was.

So the professor then picked up a box of pebbles and poured them into the jar. He shook the jar lightly. The pebbles rolled into the open areas between the rocks. He again asked the students if the jar was full. They cautiously agreed that it was.

The professor next picked up a small container of sand and poured it into the jar. Of course, the sand filled up everything else. He asked once more if the jar was full. The students responded with a unanimous "yes."

The professor then produced a can of beer from under the table and poured the entire can into the jar, effectively filling the empty space between the sand. The students laughed.

"Now," said the professor, as the laughter subsided, "I want you to recognize that this jar represents your life".

"The rocks are the important things – your family, your health, your favorite passions – things that if everything else was lost and only they remained, your life would still be full.

"The pebbles are the other things that matter – your job, your house, your car.

"The sand is everything else—the small stuff. If you put the sand into the jar first," he continued, "there is no room for the pebbles or the rocks. The same goes for life. If you spend all your time and energy on the small stuff, you'll never have room for the things that are important to you. Pay attention to the things that are critical to your happiness. Play with your children. Get medical checkups. Take your spouse out to dinner. Take a vacation. There will always be time to do the other stuff. Take care of the rocks first—the things that really matter. Set your priorities. The rest is just sand."

One of the students asked what the beer represented.

The professor smiled. "I'm glad you asked. It just goes to show you that no matter how full your life may seem, there's always room for a beer."

Each group's assignment is to identify the rocks for your organization's mayonnaise jar.

Your company's rocks should consist of the most significant areas that will be critical to taking your success to a higher level of effectiveness and profitability. These are significant issues affecting the entire organization – they are not small activities that are important to a couple of people.

By this point in the planning process, the priorities are becoming self evident, so give the participants about 30 minutes to reach consensus in their small group on what they believe the priorities should be.

There will be at least three priorities – usually these three are issues relating to money, people and operations.

There should not be more than seven priorities. If you end up with more than seven priorities, you're probably making the mistake of listing small, tactical activities that are actually subsets of larger, strategic initiatives. It's also hard to remember and focus on more than seven priorities, and we want the entire organization focused on the core priorities. Remember, you want to put a name on big items that represent your organization's rocks. For now, simply label your rocks – don't worry about making a sentence or using any verbs (we'll do that later). For now, you just want the groups to agree on the areas that provide the most significant opportunity to improve your effectiveness and profitability. Typically, these priorities have names or labels like this:

- Financial or Money or Revenue & Profit or Cash
- People – Hire, Train, Retain
- Organizational structure
- Systems & Procedures
- Communications
- Technology
- Research & Development (R&D) or the next big-selling product

Sometimes, there's a particular event in the not too distant future that is a priority. Such events can include:

- An acquisition or merger
- The sale, spin-off or closing of an office

- Geographic expansion
- New product introduction
- New service offering
- Certification of a business process
- Retirement of a key executive
- New credit facility
- Planned IPO (initial public offering)

If the group foresees a significant event in the life of the organization, be sure to list that event as a priority.

Once each group has completed this exercise, bring the small groups back together and ask each group to report their conclusions, writing their priorities on a flip chart.

Repeat this process until all of the small groups have reported their conclusions.

The beauty of this process is that the groups will see quite clearly several areas of overlap from one group to the next. They may have said it differently, but usually, the general direction and intent are in alignment. Your priorities are beginning to be established.

Once all groups have reported back to the larger group, work to reach consensus on the most important organizational priorities.

The remainder of this exercise will take about an hour. The entire exercise will take about 90 minutes.

Exercise #3

How Will You Get There?

"The road to success is always under construction."
~ Lily Tomlin

You've clearly defined your vision and established your organization's priorities.

You have direction. Your plan is beginning to take shape.

You and your leadership team will be making changes to help you achieve your vision.

As a result of the planning process, you soon will be applying a mix of proven practices and new approaches. You will be addressing some of your existing problems from a new perspective, and pursuing new opportunities using tried and true methods. You'll be doing more of some things, less of others. Starting certain activities, stopping others.

Now it's time to commit your thinking to paper.

To begin establishing a reasonable scope of work and action plan, use the findings from the previous exercises and questions. You've already answered decisively lots of key questions. Complete the planning template for Year 1 on the following page using these headings and categories – and, yes, more questions – as guidelines.

Divide the group into smaller work groups. [After completing this page, we'll be dividing into small groups one last time to complete the next-to-last planning exercise of the day.]

The planning template each small group will use is called a Migration Plan because it depicts how your organization will migrate from its current state of being to a new state of being one year, two years, and three years into the future. It's obvious that you and your team cannot implement the changes you're contemplating in your plan overnight. Change won't happen like a light switch being flicked on. The changes will take time.

This one-page plan reflects that reality, and helps everyone get a clearer picture of the areas in your organization where change will occur.

A word of warning: It's unlikely that you and your team will have all of the information you would like at your fingertips for this exercise. That's okay. And don't view this step as a budget exercise. We'll develop budgets once we've agreed on the actions required to achieve our priorities.

Yes, we want each group to be as specific as possible, but it's not realistic to expect all of the i's to be dotted and t's crossed at this point. Collin Powell, former U.S. Secretary of State and an effective Army officer, uses a two-part process to determine how much information is required to make a good decision. "Use the formula P = 40-70, in which P stands for the probability of success and the numbers indicate the percentage of information acquired. Once the information is in the 40 to 70 range," he says, "go with your gut." That's what we're looking for at this point. Whatever additional information you need to gather – confirming financials, researching competitive threats, surveying customers, etc. – can be incorporated as action items in your final plan.

The primary purpose of completing this Migration Plan at this point in the planning process is to gain general agreement on overall direction. We want you to answer *Where are you?* and *Where are you going?*

Revenue/profits – What does our financial picture look like? What do we want it to look like 12 months from now? 24 months from now? 36 months from now? If we have divisions or different business units, what will be the share of overall revenue and profit among these units?

Strategic Focus & Vision – Where are 80% of our company's time, money and energy being focused currently? Based on our priorities, where will those same resources be focused

12 months from now? 24 months from now? 36 months from now?

Major challenges – What are they now? Don't sugarcoat things. Unless we name the challenge, we cannot meet it. What will the challenges of our company be in 12 months? 24 months? 36 months?

Infrastructure Changes – What structures, operating environment, processes and financial procedures currently exist? What must they become 12 months from now? 24 months from now? 36 months from now?

Personnel Issues – What values, expertise, policies and procedures currently exist with respect to personnel? How are our current leadership needs being met? What skills and talents must we have in place 12 months from now? 24 months from now? 36 months from now?

Sales & Marketing issues – To achieve our vision, we fully understand who we want as customers. Who are we now targeting? What is our message? What channels/methods are being used to reach these persons? What must our activities in these areas become in 12 months? In 24 months? In 36 months?

Measurement changes – How will we measure our progress and effectiveness? How will we report our performance?

Use this tool to help you and your team move from your current state toward new levels of success. Remember S.M.A.R.T. Goals so that the items you list on the chart are Specific, Measurable, Attainable, Results-driven, and Time-based with deadlines.

A sample of a completed Year 1 Migration Plan is shown in the Appendix.

Give each group at least one hour to complete their Migration Plan. If more time is needed, that's okay, but keep the groups moving.

When each group is finished, re-assemble and ask each group to present to the entire team. Doing so underscores priorities, calls attention to certain specific commitments, exposes blind spots and continues to build consensus.

The entire exercise and discussion will take between two and two-and-a-half hours.

What's important to remember about this next exercise is that annual plans dissolve when goals are abstract. Or when you find yourself or your team regularly living in the past and dreaming in the future. Or when you don't set your attitude to make the required changes.

Year 1

Migration Element	Moving From... (Current State)	Moving To... (Future State)
Revenue Split ($$ + %) Profit Split ($$ + %)		
Strategic Focus		
Major Challenges		
Infrastructure Changes • Structure, Operating Environment, Processes, Financial Administration, etc.		
Personnel Changes • Values, Expertise, Policies, Procedures, Staffing needs, etc.		
Sales & Marketing Changes • Channels, Markets, Customers, Message, Materials, etc.		
Measurement Changes • Metrics, Reports, etc.		

Exercise #4

What Specific Action Must You Take?

"When all is said and done, more is said than done."
~ Lou Holtz

The Migration Plan you just completed provides you and your team with yet another level of specificity.

This specificity is critical to increasing your chances of winning on a sustained, consistent basis.

Most plans fail because of lack of follow-through and accountability. My experience has been that most people are willing to do their jobs. They want to succeed at what they've been asked to do. The problem is that specificity and clarity are lacking. They simply don't know *exactly* what constitutes success. Other times, good, capable people are asked to do things for which they're not qualified.

I've seen productive planning meetings disintegrate into nothingness by a lack of follow-through. When this happens, look no farther than the CEO to blame. It's the CEO's responsibility to convert planning into action. If you know that follow-through is not your strongest trait, bring in a third-party to help you make sure the right things are getting done.

I've also seen highly motivated leadership teams begin moving forward to implement their plan, but because clarity is missing from the specific action items, the team thinks it's scored a touchdown and is trading high-fives with one another, while the coach – AKA you, the CEO – think the ball's still on the 20-yard line. When that happens, both you and your team will be disappointed.

When thinking about what must be done, keep in mind who should do it.

Jim Buchanan, CEO of Buchanan Associates, uses a model he calls a "triad" to assemble teams in departments and for projects in his 400-person IT company. This approach matches an individual's skill to the job to be done and is based on the belief that no single person is capable of excelling at the three facets that comprise a successful engagement in his organization. It also reinforces the notion that leaders should play to peoples' strengths and manage around their weaknesses. You're mostly wasting time trying to improve a person's weakness – it's better to acknowledge the weakness and compensate for it with a second or third person who's strong in that area than asking the first person to do something that's not their strength.

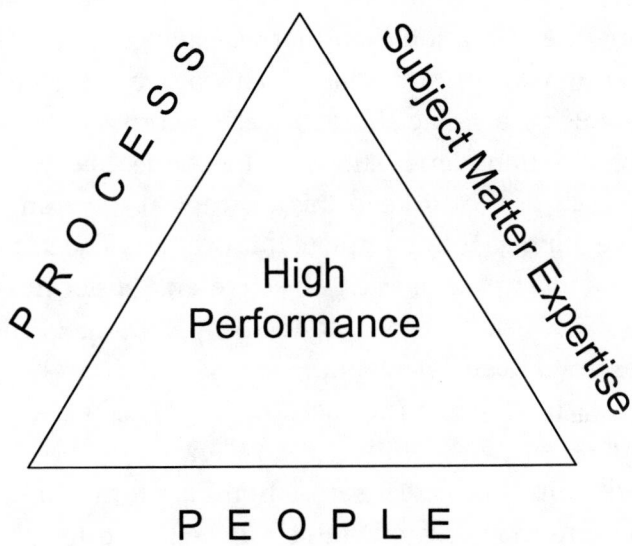

As the diagram suggests, one person is a subject matter expert who is responsible for providing or overseeing the successful development of the work itself; a second person, the "process" person, ensures that the work is being done according to the systems, procedures, and timelines that drive efficiency and effectiveness; the third person, the "people" person, is responsible for guaranteeing customer satisfaction as well as maintaining excellent working relationships among colleagues.

It's a model to keep in mind as you start to think more specifically about who will do what.

The Action Plan template on page 231 in the Appendix moves your thinking from the specificity of the Migration Plan to an even more detailed level. It's granular. When adhered to, it's a foolproof method for getting the right things done because everyone responsible for a task knows exactly what must be done, by whom, by when and for what expected outcome.

Divide the group into smaller work teams of at least four people each.

Using the Migration Plan that was just completed and the sheet listing your priorities, ask each team to complete the Action Plan using a single sheet for each priority. [A sample of a completed Action Plan is shown in the Appendix.]

Tell each group to keep this concept at the front of their collective mind as they complete this exercise: The importance, urgency and impact of each objective and supporting action item is directly proportional to the people, budgets and deadlines assigned to achieve them.

Give each work team at least 30 minutes and up to one hour to complete the pages of the Action Plan.

On the flip chart, create an Action Plan form similar to the one each group is using. Do this for the first priority, and list the priority at the top of the page just as it has been listed on the Action Plan sheet. Remember to give your priority a specific, measurable outcome and a deadline.

Once each small group has completed an Action Plan for each of the organization's agreed-upon priorities, bring the teams back together into a single group.

Ask each team to present their plan and write their action items, person responsible and deadline for each priority in the appropriate columns on the flip chart. Once the first small group has presented, ask for input from the remaining groups.

Add new action steps and modify previous action steps, responsibilities and deadlines as appropriate.

Create a new page for each priority. Repeat the process until all priorities have been presented, and action plans for each priority have been developed.

This portion of the exercise will take an hour. The entire exercise will take 90 minutes to two hours to complete.

Congratulations. Your planning work is almost done.

Almost – because there's one more crucial half-hour to go.

Turn the page for exercises to wrap up the last 30 minutes of your planning session.

"Long is the road from conception to completion."

~ Molière

9

Final 30 Minutes
of the Second Day

You've reached the last 30 minutes of your two-day planning session.

In the opening pages of this book, we called the first 90 minutes of the first day and the last 30 minutes of the second day the two most important blocks of time you and your team will spend together.

Everything that happens in between depends on these two hours.

The first 90 minutes of the first day set the tone for a process that confirmed your company's mission, vision and direction, defined success, established a specific plan to achieve success and gained alignment among the leadership team on this course of action.

All this has been accomplished. You and your team have traveled far together.

Still, your plan is nothing more than a concept. You have yet to implement a single idea during the last two days. The journey along this new road you have charted for your company is only beginning.

The final 30 minutes will determine whether the plan you and your team spent two days developing will be implemented and drive the improvement you expect your plan to help deliver.

The good news and the bad news at this point in the day is that your team is starting to get jumpy.

They're jumpy because they realize they've accomplished a lot and they're excited about it, and that's the good news. The bad news is that they're jumpy because they're also ready to leave. They've been virtual captives the last two days and they're getting restless. This jumpiness is more pronounced if your last day of planning falls on a Friday. Participants are ready to get out of the meeting room to address urgent business matters. Those that are traveling are ready to start their dash to their planes, trains and automobiles for their journey home. Everyone – perhaps even you – is ready to start the weekend.

But first you have four unfinished pieces of business to address in order to make your investment of time begin to pay dividends in the future.

And all four items can be addressed if you and your team will stay focused for 30 more minutes.

Unfinished Business

"Thinking is easy, acting is difficult, and to put one's thoughts into action is the most difficult thing in the world."

~ Goethe

Here are the four pieces of unfinished business that you and your team must now complete in 30 minutes:

- Parking Lot items
- Pledge of Accountability
- Scheduling the accountability meetings
- Adjourning the session

First, review the items listed on your Parking Lot page or pages.

It's been my experience that the planning process will have addressed most if not all of the items and issues listed on the Parking Lot pages. Confirm this.

Ask the Parking Lot Attendant to stand at the sheet and – with a red marker in hand – read off the items, one by one. As each item is read, confirm that the issue has been addressed. If it has, place a check mark by the issue to indicate it's been completed.

If there are any parking lot items that remain unresolved, gain agreement on whether a particular issue is still relevant or not. If it's no longer relevant because of other decisions reached during the planning session, mark off that item.

If an item still needs to be addressed or completed, determine whether the issue should be incorporated as an action item in your action plan. Either it should or it shouldn't. If it shouldn't, cross it off the list. If it should, write it down as an action step – complete with a person responsible for handling it, a deadline and an expected outcome.

This brief exercise shows that questions, problems, disagreements and opportunities that arose at some point during the two-day planning session now have been clarified, dismissed or assigned as specific action items to be addressed and completed in the coming weeks. You and your team have taken another step toward putting your thoughts into action. And that's another step closer to increasing your effectiveness.

This exercise will complete your Parking Lot list. It's a step that should take no more than five or six minutes.

Exercise #5

Pledge of Accountability

"Our chief want in life is somebody who shall make us do what we can."

~ **Emerson**

Throughout the planning process, you and your team have worked diligently to ensure that all of the significant issues requiring discussion were brought into the open for candid discussion. This level of trust and respect became a cornerstone of achieving alignment philosophically, strategically, financially and operationally as you developed your plan.

Now that your plan has been committed to writing, it's time to commit to one another that you will begin the hard work of implementing your plan.

Accountability can be challenging. It's why the final section of this book is devoted to systems and tools that will propel implementation and hold people accountable for their performance. When you and your team return to work after spending two days in this planning session, you must each begin to turn your thoughts into action. You must begin to turn your investment of time into profit.

Nothing will sap the energy of your team quicker than getting their hopes up and then not following through.

Ancient Greek commanders torched their ships after landing in a new land to fight an enemy on its home turf. The message to the troops was clear: *We've made our decision. There's no turning back. We're committed to victory.* Human nature hasn't changed much over thousands of years, so if your troops sense you're not committed to following through to implement your plan, they'll believe there will always be an opportunity to turn back if the changes don't work. That type of attitude will kill any type of change initiative before it's had any real chance to succeed.

Ask your team for input for ways to ensure implementation.

The decisions you make now will mark the difference between the success and failure of your plan.

How will we ensure accountability? What will be the rewards? What will be the penalties?

Accountability Meetings

Remember your commitment to invest 73 hours a year of your time to developing and implementing your written plan? You've already invested 17 hours. The commitment you and your team must now make to one another is to meet for two hours twice a month to review the progress of your plan. Agree on a day and time that will become a standing mandatory meeting, and ask everyone to place this block of time on their calendar for the next year. A block of time that I've seen work well in companies is picking two days per month to meet from 11 a.m. to 1 p.m. over a working lunch, but you and your team should agree on what works best for you.

Consequences

We'll examine in Chapter 11 the importance of consequences, so let's address only briefly the concept of establishing consequences.

The origin of the word consequence is two Latin words – *Con* (originally *com*), meaning "together" and *sequens*, meaning "to follow." It's a neutral word meaning "something that logically or naturally follows from an action or condition." Somewhere along the way, consequences have come to be viewed as unfavorable when in fact a consequence can be favorable or unfavorable.

If policies are already in place to address positive performance and under-performance, congratulations. Skip to the section entitled Pledge of Accountability. If these policies are not in place, or they are not being followed, read on.

My experience facilitating leadership teams in planning sessions is that developing a policy with rewards and penalties will need to be assigned as an action item and completed outside the planning session.

Nevertheless, here are some initial thoughts about consequences.

Determine together the rewards for achieving milestones in your plan. Doing so may require taking a second look at compensation programs. People may move for money, but what generally first pushes people toward the door is but a feeling that the work they do is either not interesting, not important or both. Your mission and vision will give them something to work for. Recognition, as we'll see in Chapter 11, is another powerful motivator for keeping employees happy, productive and engaged. For now, write down initial ideas about ways to reward individuals, departments and the company as a whole for reaching important milestones. Decide if some sort of recognition initiative needs to be added to your action plan as part of one of your priorities.

It's just as important to determine the penalties for substandard performance. Every organization will have a different view of this type of action – three strikes and you're out, a 90-day probation for habitual laggards, trimming the bottom 5% of the workforce each year based on annual performance objectives, etc. You need to determine your policy or re-commit to enforcing the one that already exists. Just like rewards, if this item needs to be added to your action plan, assign the responsibility to a specific person along with a deadline and a description of the outcome.

This discussion should take about 15 minutes so don't get bogged down in specifics. Save the specific issues that must be addressed for the action plan and subsequent implementation.

Pledge of Accountability

Next, develop and sign a written Pledge of Accountability. A sample is included in the Appendix.

This step may sound corny, but it works. Why?

First, it's a contract. You have just agreed as a leadership team that achievements will be recognized and sub-standard performance will be penalized. The reality is that peer pressure will be the motivating factor for each participant to carry out his or her commitment. Leaders, I've found, don't want to let their peers down. Or themselves.

Second, the Pledge of Accountability is a visible symbol of the team's commitment to execute the plan that's been developed. Most leadership teams that I work with mount the flip chart sheet on fiber board and display it prominently in their office – an employee break room, by a time clock, or sometimes by the front door. Some teams frame their Pledge. However you decide to preserve it and wherever you decide to place it, it's a constant reminder of the commitment to carry out the plan.

This Pledge becomes one more way each leader commits to fulfilling his or her potential. And as your leaders fulfill their potential, so, too, does your company.

The issue of positive and negative consequences must be decided within 30 days for two primary reasons. First, if it's not decided in a timely manner, it's highly likely that the decision will continue to be postponed. Postponing a decision about how to reward and penalize performance is literally the death knell to your plan. Second, you and your team will need to reach consensus on a policy concerning accountability within 30 days because the 30-day period following your planning session is where the greatest likelihood of missed deadlines occurs.

Adjourning

"The test of a first-rate intelligence is the ability to hold two opposed ideas in the mind at the same time and still retain the ability to function."

~ F. Scott Fitzgerald

The clock is ticking and there are only a few minutes left in your planning session.

Ask for a volunteer or assign a participant to take responsibility for transcribing all flip chart pages into a single document to capture the notes from your planning session.

These pages will include but are not limited to notes from all the exercises, diagrams, schematics, tables, quotes, etc. Above all, make sure to capture the pages that will form the backbone of your plan:

- Vision
- Corporate essence (Indentity Pyramid)
- Competitive Advantage
- Migration Plan
- Priorities & action plan
- Pledge of Accountability

Set a deadline for distributing the notes to all participants for their review to ensure everything that's already been agreed upon is represented accurately. Make every effort to set the deadline for distributing the notes to participants no later than one week from the last day of your planning session, otherwise the momentum you built during these two days will begin to dissipate. This step will take one minute.

Repeat the feedback exercise at the end of yesterday's planning session by recording on a flip chart what your leaders felt was high value and what they would like to see changed the next time the group meets. This exercise should take just three or four minutes.

You've now concluded the business portion of the day.

With only four or five minutes left in your day, it becomes your responsibility as the leader of leaders to adjourn the planning session.

Your concluding remarks should contain these three elements:

1. Thank the leadership team for giving up time away from the business. For those that spent time away from their homes, thank them for their personal time as well. Thank the facilitator if you're happy with his or her work.

2. Commend the group on its thoughtful, respectful and honest participation. Express your enthusiasm for what has been accomplished as a team, most notably:

   • Underscoring company values

   • Addressing candidly issues requiring discussion

   • Agreeing upon a vision, direction and priorities

   • Developing a specific action plan, and

   • Strengthening relationships

3. Temper the enthusiasm with the sober reminder that the situation back at the ranch will be largely unchanged from where you left it two days ago. The challenge, therefore, will be to face the realities of the present while remaining focused on, committed to and excited about the future each participant worked these last two days to create. It is their responsibility as smart leaders to hold these "two opposed ideas" – the reality of the present as well as the potential of the future – in their minds once they return to work.

   If you want to read a quote that strikes you as particularly pertinent, go ahead and do so. But as Franklin Roosevelt said, "be sincere, be brief and be seated."

Your planning session is complete.

Now comes the hard part – implementation.

Take Action

Write the date for distributing the notes from the planning session to all participants in the space below.

_____

Now, using a scale of 1 – 10 (with 10 the top score), rate your two-day planning session and write why you gave it that score.

_____

_____

_____

_____

Turn back to the end of Chapter 3 and compare your thoughts right now with the benefits you wanted to receive or outcomes you wanted to achieve from this planning session. How do your thoughts today compare with your earlier thoughts? Did your expectations change? If so, how? Why?

_____

_____

Part 3

*There is nothing more difficult
to take in hand, more perilous to
conduct, or more uncertain
in its success than to take the
lead in the introduction
of a new order of things.*

~ Niccolo Machiavelli

...Go!

"Good business leaders create a vision,
articulate the vision,
passionately own the vision
and relentlessly drive it to completion."

~ Jack Welch

10

Moving Forward

You're back in your office and struck with the thought that nothing's changed.

In some respects, you're right. Nothing happens just because we say it or write it down.

It's true you and your leaders invested valuable time to reflect on the past and plan for the future. You addressed some significant issues. Even those issues that you already knew how you'd handle have now been embraced by your leadership team. You're all on the same page.

But the planning's over. You're back at work and you find the same obstacles, dilemmas and distractions waiting for you.

What's really different?

For starters, your attitude. You should feel encouraged by the progress you and your team made during your two-day planning session. You accomplished more in two days than you thought was possible. There was zero wasted time.

And now you have a plan with specific action items that you and your team will begin implementing. Your team is aligned around the vision as well as the action that must be accomplished to achieve that vision.

In our microwavable society, we want our wishes to be satisfied immediately. That's not realistic, especially when you think about implementing your plan. Implementing your plan will take time and discipline. Think of the process of raising and sustaining your organization's performance as a continuing journey:

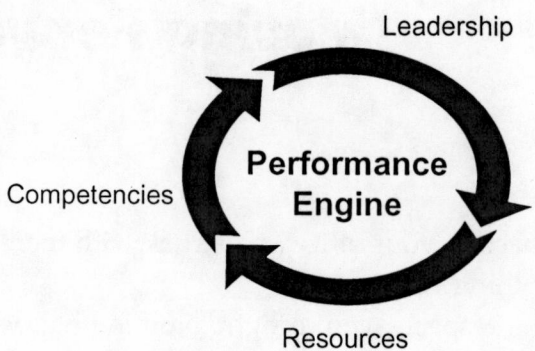

Continue your journey and start moving forward to implement your plan by first focusing on these four items:

- Establish your personal time management system

- Turn the notes from the planning session into a plan

- Announce the results of planning to your entire company

- Lead the first post-planning accountability meeting

True change must start at the top before it can be embraced throughout a company.

Establish Your Personal Time Management System

"Lost: Yesterday, somewhere between Sunrise and Sunset, two golden hours, each set with sixty diamond minutes. No reward is offered, for they are gone forever."

~ Horace Mann

As a leader, you must be discerning and disciplined. About the company's focus. About the execution of your plan. And about your own time.

What type of time management system will you use to help you execute your plan effectively on a daily basis?

Not sure? Go back and review the three time management techniques in Chapter 8. If you don't like any of those, that's fine. Create your own. Or ask a fellow CEO how he or she manages time and try out theirs. Just get a system that you like and will continue to use.

As you adopt, adapt or create your own time management system, take a few minutes to complete the CEO versus COO exercise in the Appendix. Now think back to the things you said at the start of the second day of planning that you committed to start doing consistently and stop doing consistently in order to make yourself more effective.

Write those things down – I recommend posting them in your office, making them part of your screen saver, putting them on your PDA or wherever you keep your calendar – so that you can refer to them repeatedly. It can be effective to post your list where your leadership team can see them so that they know you're committed to following through on the promise you made.

How you handle your Start/Stop issues this week will determine whether or not you have adjusted your mindset to do what needs to be done to improve. Are you willing to discipline yourself to focus on the activities that give you and your company the highest return on your investment of time?

Got your time management system?

You better. Because here come the next three priorities that you must accomplish in the first week following your planning session.

Take Action

Complete the CEO versus COO exercise in the Appendix. Write the specific action you will take to increase your effectiveness as a CEO along with a deadline for completing the action.

_____

_____

_____

_____

_____

Turn the Notes into a Plan

> *"Those who dream by night...awake to find that it was vanity. But the dreamers of the day may act their dream with open eyes to make it possible."*
> ~ T. E. Lawrence (Lawrence of Arabia)

In the final 30 minutes of the planning session, a member of your leadership team volunteered or was assigned by you to transcribe the notes from the two-day session.

A deadline was set for distributing the notes to all participants.

Check with the person who's handling this task to ensure the deadline will be met. I'm assuming it will be. After all, if you and your team have trouble meeting this simple deadline, following through to implement the plan you just developed will be even more of a challenge.

Once the notes have been approved, the actual plan will be lifted straight from the notes.

In Chapter 5, I suggested that your plan need not be more than 10 to 20 pages.

The reason for the brevity is simple: Most of us are exposed to so much information that we have a hard time remembering it all unless that information is whittled down to the most important facts. A dashboard approach that zeroes in on your priorities and the specific action items for achieving the desired objectives is the way to go.

Instruct the person responsible for transcribing the notes to take one more step and reduce the notes into your plan.

Your completed written plan will consist of these pages:

- Cover sheet with your company's logo, a title and a date

- Vision statement

- Identity Pyramid

- Competitive Advantage

- Priorities

- Migration Plan

- Action plan – there will be anywhere from 3 pages to a dozen, depending upon the number of priorities and the number of action items listed for each priority; convert the priorities into measurable objectives [if you want to combine the priorities page(s) with the acion plan pages, that's fine]

- Pledge of Accountability

All the other pages of notes are back-up and do not need to be incorporated into your plan.

Don't discard them. You may want to refer to them as you move forward with implementation.

The path to winning is now in the hands of you and your leadership team.

Before distributing the final plan, call a company-wide meeting to announce the results of your planning session.

Take Action

Set a date for a company-wide announcement and write it in the space below. Now commit to a deadline for writing and distributing a company-wide email with the particulars of the meeting, and inviting all employees to attend or tune in.

_____

_____

_____

_____

_____

Announce the Results

> "If you are planning for a year, sow rice; if you are plan-
> ning for a decade, plant trees; if you are planning for a
> lifetime, educate people."
>
> ~ Chinese proverb

No matter the size of your company, those that did not have the opportunity to participate in the two-day planning session will be interested to learn what happened when all of the company's leaders convened to discuss the future.

It is your responsibility to tell them.

It is also your opportunity to inspire them.

You don't need to be a so-called visionary or loaded with charisma to inspire your troops. What's important is determining how to make the most of changes that may already be occurring in or around your organization and then executing the plan you and your leadership team have just developed. Actions speak louder than words, and your employees will be eager to hear the specifics of how the company is going to move from point A to point B.

Whether you are able to gather everyone in a single location or you must rely on technology to reach employees in remote locations simultaneously, schedule a 30-minute meeting well enough in advance so that the chances of total participation is high. You'll probably never be able to get every single employee in one place at once, so don't worry about it. More on that later.

How you choose to communicate is largely a matter of your style and your company's culture.

If you're comfortable speaking from notes, use them. If you'd like to walk your employees through a PowerPoint presentation, that's fine, too.

There should be two components of your remarks: Information and inspiration.

Briefly explain who was invited to the strategic planning session and why, explain that the results you are about to share was accomplished through a lot of hard work in two intense days that was completed just a matter of days ago.

It's important that your employees know that no topics were off limits, that differences of opinion were handled with honesty and respect, and that the entire leadership team is 100% supportive of this plan.

Tell – and show – them that you are enthusiastic about the future.

Focus on the elements of the plan. Depending upon your style and your company's culture, you should cover these points from the plan:

- Who you are as an organization – your values (Identity Pyramid)

- Your competitive advantage

- Your vision

- Your priorities

- A [number]-page plan with [number] action items to accomplish those priorities has been developed

- Explain in broad terms things that are not changing and some of the key things that are

- Supervisors will be meeting with employees to answer questions and describe in full the implications to your respective department and to you and the work you're doing

- The leadership team will meet twice a month to review progress on the plan, and that you expect to see progress [be specific] on certain priorities by [date]

- You are personally committed to the successful implementation of the plan, and that you are counting on each employee to play a role in the future success of the company

Now is not the time to sugarcoat any obstacles that must be overcome in order to turn your vision into a reality.

Acknowledge the realities, but emphasize that the newly developed plan takes these difficulties into account. Tell your employees what you expect and explain any new ground rules and code of conduct under which the organization will operate as it moves forward. Let your people know the challenges you face as an organization. Help them understand the pivotal role they play and that you expect them to get the job done well – even on those days when they don't feel like it. Communicate your new or renewed commitment to equip and train them to be the best at what they do. Finally, help them understand the consequences of acceptable and unacceptable performance.

Don't underestimate your employees' desire to accept a challenge.

Consider the following ad:

> Men Wanted for Hazardous Journey. Small wages, bitter cold, long months of complete darkness, constant danger, safe return doubtful. Honor and recognition in case of success.

The ad was written by polar explorer Sir Ernest Shackleton and appeared in London newspapers in 1900. The response was overwhelming. The ad was effective because it appealed to men who desired honor and recognition and because of its candor and simplicity.

The lesson: When you have the right people, tell them exactly what you want them to accomplish and what to expect if they achieve the objective. How they respond should please you, not surprise you.

At the end of your remarks – which should take no more than 20 minutes – ask for questions.

Stay focused on linking your answers back to your vision and your plan for achieving it.

When you've reached the 30-minute mark, thank everyone for their time and attention and adjourn the meeting. Be respectful of taking no more than 30 minutes for this meeting. It's another lesson in making productive use of time, and it's another indication of doing what you say you're going to do.

If there are any other questions, invite people to discuss these with the leaders that participated in the planning meeting or to ask you directly.

Because it's likely that not everyone will be able to attend the company-wide meeting, write and send immediately a brief e-mail to all employees summarizing your presentation.

Your e-mail offers the added benefit of reinforcing your remarks to those that heard you the first time. If you have an employees-only space on your company's website, consider posting your presentation or remarks there, too. Doing so allows people to review your presentation. For companies with warehouses and shop floor operations, post the priorities in visible locations. Use visuals to illustrate points if language barriers exist.

Now your entire organization knows the plan.

The next step is to check the progress that's beginning to be made on your priorities.

Take Action

Assess your delivery. List three things you believe you did well and list three areas where you can improve the next time you address your team.

_____

_____

_____

_____

Next, solicit feedback privately from each member of your leadership team. Ask each leader to name one thing they thought you did well and one area where you can improve. How does their assessment compare to yours? If their assessment differs greatly from yours, what do these differences suggest?

_____

_____

_____

Lead the First Post-Planning
Accountability Meeting

*"When building a team, I first look for people who love to
win. If I can't find any of those, then I look for people who
hate to lose."*

~ Ross Perot

This two-hour meeting is the first of 24 meetings you and your
team will be spending together for the coming 12 months for
the sole purpose of tracking your plan's implementation.

You can make the call about whether to circle up as a team
one week after the planning session, or to schedule the first
meeting two weeks later. I suggest meeting one week later because there's enough on the agenda to warrant it. Plus, doing
so helps maintain the momentum you achieved coming out of
your two-day planning session.

Your first step in the accountability meeting is to commit
to your leaders that this accountability meeting will not take
more than two hours – today and in the future. [You'll recall
that scheduling these meetings from 11 a.m. to 1 p.m. over
a working lunch kills two birds with one stone. You have to
eat lunch, right? Might as well eat while you're reviewing the
progress of your plan.]

Next, go around the table – just like at the planning session
– and ask each leader to share two pieces of information. Unlike at the planning session, you should address the first issue
yourself, though you should hold on addressing the second issue until everyone else has spoken. Give everyone one minute
to briefly describe:

- The time management system each person is now using,
and

- A comment or perspective following your address to the
entire company regarding the vision and the plan.

Doing this serves five purposes:

1. It gives everyone a chance to participate. You are modeling behavior the group learned in the planning session.

2. This is a lesson in time management. Train your people to be disciplined, organized, and concise. We don't need a speech from everyone. We just want to hear quickly from everyone in the room.

3. It's the first of many lessons in discipline and accountability. As will be emphasized repeatedly in the remainder of this book, what gets measured is what gets done. You must continue to track performance on the things that matter to you. Did your leaders do what they committed to do or not?

4. Inevitably, one of your leaders will admit that the press of business and getting caught up after being out two days left him or her no time to figure out a time management system. How you and the group address this matter sets the tone for future performance lapses that may occur in the future. Do not treat this matter lightly. Make it visible to the group. Ask if the person's accountability partner reminded him or her of the commitment. Decide as a group the consequences of non-compliance.

5. This will be your early indicator of feedback in terms of how the troops are responding to the company's direction and its course of action.

Turning to the plan, take each of the priorities in order. Focus on the action items with upcoming deadlines and ask those who are responsible for the completing the action items for a brief report.

Tell your leaders that you want to hear three things from them when they report on the status of action items:

1. Completed work and the outcome

2. Any change in deadlines – accelerating, lagging and why

3. Any help team members need from those in the room, including you

Since only a week has gone by since adjourning the planning session, there may not be much movement on the action items. That's okay. You are modeling behavior you'll be using at subsequent meetings. If you choose to meet two weeks after your planning session, your expectations should be higher in terms of the initial progress made thus far.

While you may have action items of your own, your primary job is to lead and equip those around you so that they can complete their action items. You're an enabler. You're in the barrier removal business. You're a sounding board. And you're always asking questions to make sure your leaders know you are engaged, helpful and committed to the execution of the plan.

If you complete your first post-planning accountability in less than two hours, so much the better.

Before adjourning the meeting, use the feedback exercise from the two-day planning session to learn from each of your leaders what they found to be valuable about the meeting. Write down their comments. Ask them what they found to be of little value or what changes should be considered to make the next accountability meeting in two weeks even more productive. [Repeat this exercise after each accountability meeting; the process will likely go more quickly at each subsequent meeting, but you should never stop asking for feedback.]

Thank everyone for their time and adjourn the meeting.

You and your leadership team have begun moving forward with the hard work of implementation by completing key actions that you committed to complete when you developed your plan.

You're on your way.

Take Action

Review the comments from your leaders and list the action you will take to make the next accountability meeting even more productive for all participants.

Getting Smarter

"As a general rule, the most successful man in life is the one who has the best information."

~ Benjamin Disraeli

During the two-day planning process, a premium was placed on "possibility thinking."

We noted that attitudes expressed as *We've never done that before* and *We've always done it this way* would hold back creativity and new thinking.

We agreed that there would be an appropriate time later for analysis, reason and judgment to determine if a possibility can become a probability.

That time is now.

In some cases, it's an opportunity to determine if an idea is workable. In other cases, it's simply a matter of doing more homework or gathering more information so that an informed decision can be made. In both cases, budgets must be prepared to match the priorities that have been established.

Some issues requiring further study are strategic, such as

expanding into a territory, offering a new product or service, or acquiring a competitor. Others are operational, such as reducing your supplier relationships, adjusting your compensation program or establishing a new banking resource.

I'm assuming both types of issues were raised in your discussion and addressed in your action plan. Because of the planning schedule, there wasn't time to reach definitive conclusions on these issues. But it's time to gather facts and make a decision.

Let's take a quick look at ways to gather data.

What you might not realize is that fully three-quarters of the information you need to understand your competitors (and therefore your customers) is publicly available. Yet according to a market study by Knowledge Systems & Research, 87 percent of business leaders consider gathering intelligence information to support decisions and to develop and maintain winning strategies a major challenge.

Traditionally, the gathering of competitive intelligence in the business world has focused on competitive threats, most often in the form of direct competitors battling inch-by-inch for market share and, for those companies left standing, market dominance.

But business leaders operating in a changing or uncertain environment must think more broadly than simply how they stack up to their competitors. There's no guarantee that those competitors will be real threats a year from now or that the business environment will be the same.

Competitive intelligence (or CI) is a systematic program for gathering and analyzing information about your competitors' activities and general business trends to accelerate your own business objectives. Whatever the size of your business, you'll outpace your competitors if you 1) understand how CI impacts your business; 2) know how to acquire the most helpful information; and 3) know how to use the information you acquire.

Your competitors generate enormous amounts of information that can be helpful to you in understanding your competitive environment. This information can come from your competitors' web sites, from their annual or company reports, government filings and other public domain sources. Literature searches of published sources, including newspaper articles and trade publications, also are valuable. Non-competitive sources such as industry experts, suppliers, financial analysts and academics will account for the remaining 20 percent of your intelligence gathering.

Just remember, if you can go to school on your competitors, they can go to school on you.

It's also a good idea to test the positioning statement you and your team developed to articulate your competitive advantage.

"The buyer never buys what the seller thinks he's selling," said Peter Drucker. You need to find out what your customers and prospective customers think about your claims.

Whether you gather this information yourself or retain an outside firm to do it, don't neglect this step. An outside firm that specializes in gathering this type of information can do so quickly and relatively inexpensively. An outside firm can offer anonymity and confidentiality to your customers and prospects, which will yield a greater degree of honest feedback. I've seen instances when claims made by an organization were counter-productive to achieving the sales they wanted (the company sold to distributors that sold to end-users and the company's claim threatened the distributors).

Test your assumptions. The most expensive kind of research is none.

Take Action

Think about a company with which you regularly compete. How well do you know them? What are they doing to win customers, improve their supplier relationships and attract the best talent? What can you learn from this competitor? List three specific pieces of information you'd like to learn about this competitor that has the potential to make you and your company more effective. Develop a concise plan of action to secure this information, including a person to gather the information and a deadline for completing the task.

_____

_____

_____

_____

Take Action

How will you gather feedback from customers and prospective customers to test the assumptions you've made about your organization's competitive advantage? Who will oversee this project? When will it be completed?

_____

_____

_____

_____

Getting Smart about Operational Issues

"Nothing in life is to be feared. It is only to be understood."

~ Marie Curie

Recall that in Chapter 1 it was noted that if you've not planned at all or had difficulty implementing your plans, your initial approach to planning should be to develop an annual plan.

The primary value of this type of plan is derived from getting all of your leaders focused on the most important operational issues that they and their teams will implement over the next 12 months to improve performance.

There may be some low-hanging fruit to be picked in the form of improved productivity, morale, profitability, and cash flow by researching opportunities for improvements in these nine broad areas:

- Work product development and delivery procedures

- Productivity trends, benchmarks and personal performance targets and results

- Recruiting guideline and on-boarding/exiting of employees

- Training and development resources – people, products, services (R&D)

- Compensation trends and models

- Employee recognition programs

- Customer satisfaction indices

- Supplier relationships, practices and terms

- Money matters: Cash flow, A/R, banking relationships and terms

You can achieve clarity on ways to improve operational

performance by following a process that's based on asking and answering a series of questions similar to those asked in the opening exercises of your two-day planning session: *What is our current situation? What is the gold standard for this situation? How can we apply the gold standard to our situation?*

What Is Our Current Situation?

Your first step is to assign one of your leaders to assemble the facts about what your company is or isn't doing in a particular area that you're seeking to improve.

You're looking for a baseline set of information that all of your leaders can agree accurately represent the current situation. It's also the information you will use to compare yourself to others.

What Is the Gold Standard for this Situation?

Gold standards, as you no doubt already know, are those practices, leadership qualities and business models that define the concept of excellence in the eyes of the marketplace.

In most cases, whatever situation your company must now address, another company has already addressed it.

As previously noted, there's no shortage of information available to you on this issue. Find out what other companies – inside your industry and outside your industry – have done in similar situations. What investments of time, money, talent or reputation were involved? What were the risks? The rewards? What worked? What didn't? What's the long-term effect from having taken a certain action?

These questions and others will give you and your team a good basis of comparison.

How Can We Apply the Gold Standard to Our Situation?

Compare your gold standard findings with the facts you assembled to show what you're doing (or not doing) in this area.

Doing so will provide you with an objective look at gaps, opportunities and areas requiring more information.

Encourage all team members to challenge the thinking. By challenging the idea, one of two things will happen. Either the idea will be shown to be unworkable or possible solutions to the challenges will emerge. Don't consider this step an exercise in negative thinking. Rather, it's an acknowledgement of reality.

If you still need more information, go get it. But remember Colin Powell's rule that good decisions can be made with 40 to 70 percent of the available information. There's plenty of information available. Don't get into analysis paralysis by asking your team to deliver more information.

Making the right decision is not always easy. But when you have taken the necessary steps to assess reality, you can be confident that you've made the best decision possible using the best information and input you have available to you.

Once decisions have been reached, budgets must be developed reflecting the priorities. Where a shift in priorities has occurred, budgets will need to be reduced or increased accordingly. Where new initiatives are planned, budgets will need to be developed from scratch. Set timeframes for completing your new operating budget. Your team will be watching to see if you and the company are willing to put your money where your mouth was during the planning session.

Take Action

Talk with your leaders to determine where additional learning can accelerate the improvement of one or two areas within the company. Is it sales, operations, people, systems, a new banking relationship? Where is the low-hanging fruit? Pick one area upon which to focus your information-gathering process. It's probably an action item related to one of your priorities. Once you've agreed on the area to target, assign the appropriate leader to develop a plan for acquiring the necessary information using the model discussed above. What area in your business will benefit from fresh, outside information? What could be the impact of that information?

_____

_____

_____

_____

_____

_____

_____

Getting Smart about Strategic Issues

"It's not that I'm so smart, it's just that I stay with problems longer."

~ Albert Einstein

Once you've developed and implemented an annual plan, you and your team can turn your attention in Year 2 to developing and implementing a strategic plan. Strategic planning should examine fresh opportunities that can increase your profitable growth.

It starts by asking *Where will our future profitable growth come from?*

To help focus your research and thinking, first consider the specific area of growth using the following diagram:

Geographic Expansion	Vertical Segments
Products & Services	Alliances & Acquisitions

You can achieve clarity about whether to proceed on a strategic initiative by asking and answering three deceptively simple questions to support effective decision-making: *Is the threat or opportunity real? Can we win? Will the win be worth it?*

Is It Real?

You've already articulated your vision and you've established clear, measurable objectives. So before determining if the threat or opportunity you face in your business is real, you must ask and answer how pursuing an opportunity or fighting the battle will support your strategic direction. Will the outcome benefit customers, employees, investors and other stakeholders? If the answer to either question is "no," you should abandon the idea.

Let's assume the answer is "yes." I've also assumed that the matter at hand is an opportunity and not a threat, though the process for working through the analysis of a response to a perceived threat follows the same steps.

The question *Is it real?* leads to other considerations. Here are three steps to take to help answer that question:

1. Was the opportunity raised through a customer feedback process? If not, have you tested the idea with customers? Customers are great at telling you what they like and dislike.

2. What marketplace trends have you observed? Are others offering this product or service? What are the gaps in products or services that customer and prospects say they want that no company is providing or providing at a consistently high level of quality? Gather data, analyze trend, and draw initial conclusions.

3. Does the analysis indicate there's an emerging market? Test the opportunity with outside advisors.

Can We Win?

The second key question is not simply a numbers exercise, though the financial implications play a significant role in this process. This step focuses on your company's ability to align the opportunity with your vision and the hard work of implementation. Winning in the marketplace takes more than dreaming and a great pro forma. Sure, a good idea and compelling strategy are important. But the road is littered with good ideas that, ultimately, people really didn't want or that could not be executed.

You must ask yourself if you and your organization have the skill, experience, time, drive and money to pursue the opportunity and succeed. Consider these four steps to help answer the *Can we win?* question:

1. View the situation from the outside in

2. Identify all key issues and concerns

3. Revisit the *Is it real?* answer to determine what outcome is acceptable

4. Identify possible new options that may help you achieve your desired outcome

Don't just talk about this idea with your team, go get some research to test your assumptions. You don't have to spend a lot of time or money to secure this information, at least not initially. Remember, the most expensive form of research is none.

After the financial and go-to-market scenarios are developed, incorporate the competitive information you've gathered in the *Is it real?* analysis. Taken together, the two sets of data should show – usually very clearly – whether it's possible for you to win a particular marketplace battle based on your product or service, your go-to-market strategy and your marketplace position relative to its competition.

Is It Worth It?

So you've determined the opportunity is real and that winning is possible. Now comes the toughest question. Is winning worth it? This is the time to be pragmatic and committed. Because winning requires commitment, and commitment always carries a cost.

These costs include more than money, though financial investment is certainly a consideration. *How much management time will be required to implement this initiative? What effect will management's lack of focus on other parts of the business have on performance and profitability? How will we proceed if we have underestimated our projected investments of time, money and talent? What will be the impact on morale if we pull the plug? What will be the impact on morale of a "win at all cost" approach?*

When your organization faces a key strategic decision, ask – and answer – these three fundamental questions to help drive the necessary action.

Take Action

Customers and prospects offer valuable insights into issues of strategic importance to your company. When was the last time you obtained feedback from a large, representative group of your customers and prospects? If it's been more than 18 months since your company has surveyed customers and prospects, it's been too long. Someone in your company can ask the questions, but you'll get better information if you retain an outside firm to help with this process. The firm can emphasize confidentiality and will observe patterns – both good and bad – that your team might miss. Ask a fellow CEO to recommend a research or marketing firm. Write the person's name you will talk with about his/her recommendation for a research firm. Also note the most important piece of information you want to learn from your research and a deadline for completing the research.

_____

_____

_____

_____

"What gets measured gets done; what gets recognized gets done better."

~ Anonymous

11

How Are We Doing?

As you move into the second week of implementing your plan and prepare for your bi-weekly accountability meeting, it's worth reminding your leadership team of your accomplishments. You and your team have reason to be proud of the work you've completed.

There are five more issues to address to make sure your plan is working to increase your company's effectiveness and profitability, and these five issues should be discussed at the bi-weekly (i.e., every two weeks *not* twice per week) accountability meeting. These issues are:

- Monitoring and measuring performance
- Gaining individual commitment
- Establishing consequences
- Replicating success
- Removing obstacles

It's a good idea to distribute in advance an agenda for the bi-weekly accountability meeting so that your leaders know that these issues need to be discussed and resolved in short order. I'm not suggesting that all five issues must be completed at the next accountability meeting, but I encourage you to make sure these five issues are listed as action items with deadlines on your plan because each one plays a big part in helping your company reach new levels of effectiveness.

I'm assuming that the "consequences" issue is already listed as one of your action items. Perhaps the other four issues are, too.

Let's look at each of the five issues.

Monitoring and Measuring Performance

"To him that watches, everything is revealed."
~ Italian proverb

You're now tracking the progress of your plan's implementation in your bi-weekly accountability meetings.

Doing so is essential because monitoring and measuring performance are the twin processes by which real change takes effect, reaches its full potential and becomes institutionalized within an organization.

Most plans don't fail because the ideas and initiatives in them are mediocre. Most plans fail for lack of follow-through. It's true that a mediocre plan that's implemented is better than a terrific plan that's not executed. If you're not watching to ensure that the action items in your plan are being executed according to the schedule and the level of excellence you and your team established, deadlines will be missed, quality will suffer and you will not achieve the results you expected your plan to deliver. You and your team must be disciplined.

To achieve short-term outcomes and develop a platform for sustained success, people must see how new approaches are improving performance.

Monitoring performance means that you are observing the activities that are taking place – or not taking place. You're watching the activities. When people know that leaders are paying attention to what they're doing, they tend to do a better job.

Measuring performance means that you are assigning a value to the effectiveness of the action that you observed. You're assessing the return on your investment of time, money and effort.

You should measure your effectiveness inside your organization as well as externally with your customers or clients. Measurement helps deliver customer satisfaction and career growth for employees year after year. And, most important, measurement helps drive sustained effectiveness for your organization by pinpointing performance issues.

We'll examine in greater detail in the next section approaches for securing individual commitment.

Let's take a quick look at measuring customer satisfaction.

As with any measurement process, you must start with a baseline assessment of the current situation and the scope of work to be performed or product to be delivered. Ask your customers to provide feedback on your performance or hire a third-party firm to ask the questions if anonymity is important.

Successful companies do this regularly with their customers as a matter of course – both through formalized, written evaluations and through informal, ongoing conversations between leaders of the company providing the product or service and leaders of the company that's on the receiving end. In service firms, areas for measurement include, but are not limited to, assessing your company's understanding of your client's business; an evaluation of your staff's skills, ability, accessibility and collaboration; results of the work being performed; and overall management of the relationship and the engagement. In manufacturing companies, areas for measurement include, but are not limited to, ease of doing business, including order placement, customer service and service after the sale; timeliness and accuracy of order delivery; and quality of the product being manufactured. Retailers and distribution companies can adopt versions of these questions for their particular use. In all cases, strengths and weaknesses should be noted.

For all companies that sell a product or service, the ultimate aim is to determine your customer or client's satisfaction with the value they receive from you, the likelihood of future assignments or purchases and whether there's a willingness to provide references. A candid information exchange not only pinpoints problems to fix but also can help identify new revenue opportunities. Unhappy customers, it's been observed, can provide your greatest sources for learning. Asking for and receiving customer feedback can create the platform for a long, mutually beneficial relationship.

Once you've gathered this information from your customers, assign numerical values to the data. Plot this data on a chart. You'll have a picture of your company's performance according to a certain sample of your customers. What does this picture tell you?

Introducing and then maintaining other monitoring and measurement systems in your organization can be just as simple and effective. Your measurement system needn't be onerous or time-consuming tasks.

There are a variety of off-the-shelf technology tools that can be customized to track performance and productivity, but any process – even if it's just using pen and paper – that effectively tracks productivity, drives accountability and measures results will work.

The peer pressure occurring in your bi-weekly accountability meetings are, frankly, more important than whatever technology tool you may choose to apply to help you in this process. What's important is that you must stick with it for these processes to deliver sustained results.

When it's necessary to make an exception to a previously agreed upon commitment (particularly when you're in the early stages of trying to institutionalize change), the exception should be recorded and made with the full knowledge and acceptance of the team (if it's a group goal) or the supervisor (if it's an individual goal). Be careful: Don't allow the exception to become the rule. Too many variances will kill the project or, worse, indicate to others that the deadlines that are being set and the commitments being made are negotiable or arbitrary. Balance your trust of the individual with your expectation that all commitments be met.

A disciplined approach based on a foundation of clarity and upheld by regular measurement increases significantly the likelihood of two important outcomes. One, shared expectations with customers will lead to a greater understanding of the value your team brings to their business. Two, satisfied employees with clearly established responsibilities will be more productive and, therefore, more valuable to the organization.

As you watch, question, challenge and probe in your biweekly accountability meetings, you'll begin to observe patterns in your team's performance that may be linked to larger, more systemic issues.

Here are some questions to ask as you monitor and measure your plan's implementation:

- How do you currently measure the effectiveness of your organization?

- If you were on a desert island, what Key Performance Indicators (KPIs) would you consider vital in order to run your business on a daily or weekly basis?

- What are all of the strategic levers that drive your business?

- Where is the Pareto Principle at work in your company – what is the 20% of activity that produces 80% of the results?

- What causes sales to occur in your organization?

- Do you have a system in place for regularly measuring customer or client satisfaction? When was the last time you measured satisfaction? What did it show? What did you learn?

- What tangible measures have you assigned to your most intangible company goals?

- Have you codified your processes into a common management framework?

- Are you minimizing waste, variations and errors in order to increase speed, quality and profits?

- Are you receiving the return on investment for your initiatives that you expect?

- How must we structure *ourselves* and the *company* to handle effectively the growth we want and expect?

- When your employees leave for the day, do they know whether or not they have had a successful day?

Leaders get the behavior they tolerate.

Take Action

Use the 12 questions above as an initial checklist for examining your company's performance. Place a checkmark alongside the questions you have already answered. Of the remaining questions, which ones are the most significant to answer to immediately improve your business performance? Answers to which questions will improve your long-term success? Write the specific action you will take with a deadline for completing it.

_____

_____

_____

Gaining Individual Commitment

"Individual commitment to a common effort – that's what makes a team work, a company work, a society work, a civilization work."

~ Vince Lombardi

After setting corporate and departmental objectives, now is the time to establish individual performance objectives. It's also the time to establish individual commitment.

If you're already doing this on an annual or twice-a-year basis, what's important to do at this point is to ensure that the corporate and departmental objectives are aligned with each individual's performance objectives. This may sound obvious, but remember that you and your team may have developed new priorities and placed on the back burner activities that were more important before the planning session.

It's your responsibility to build a sustainable, profitable organization, and systems and processes must be in place. Sub-par performance hobbles your team. So hold people accountable, starting with yourself.

If you've never evaluated your employees, or you have not done so consistently, it's time to take this step so that each person knows what's expected of him or her, and so that this performance can be monitored and measured.

The model below will help you consider what qualities are important in those that work in your organization. It's a reminder that skill, knowledge, and technical proficiency are only half of the components in an equation where attitude, desire, and collegiality also matter.

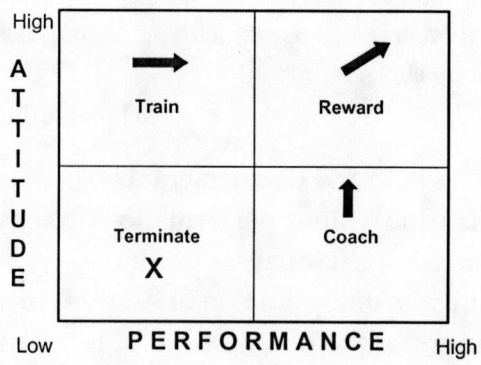

One of the toughest decisions you'll make as a leader is determining how to address employees who perform at a high level of skill but do so with poor attitudes. These people can be a cancer to your entire organization. What's more, their behavior – both good and bad – is so ingrained that it's hard for them to change. I once hired a person to supervise a team of people working on two of our firm's important accounts. Her work was stellar. She got results. The clients loved her. But she terrorized her staff. She was Dr. Jekyll with her clients and Ms. Hyde with her staff. I spoke repeatedly with her about her behavior toward her colleagues and offered coaching to correct her behavior. But when the behavior did not change, I terminated her. My phone calls to her clients who had never observed her rude behavior were difficult, but they supported my decision to let her go. Had I failed to take appropriate action, the people she supervised would ultimately have left my company, and doing nothing would've undermined my credibility among those who knew all too well what was happening.

That's why it's important to be clear and specific about what constitutes successful performance in your organization.

You can achieve this clarity by requiring all parties to commit to taking certain action to achieve their respective objectives. Do your best to make these commitments measurable, and then write them down. Without documentation, a commitment fades with memory.

Many companies that I work with make the feedback process two-way. As one part of the assessment, the supervisor assesses the work of the employee, and the employee provides a self-assessment to rate how he or she is performing against individual objectives. In addition to visiting with the employee about how he or she is doing, use the opportunity to ask the employee for his or her views on how the department is performing, how management is performing, how the company as a whole is doing. Another approach is the "360 review." As you may know, the review takes its name from the fact that there are 360 degrees in a circle, and this review solicits feedback about an employee from those – peers and subordinates, not just a supervisor – with whom the employee works.

One more word on reviews: If you can't tell by now, I favor a simple approach. The fewer items you ask an employee to focus on, the more likely those items will be upper most in the mind of the employee, increasing the chances of effectiveness. Asking someone to "focus" on 10 or 12 or 20 "areas for improvement" is not focus at all. A simple test for employee productivity is to determine if every single employee can say whether or not they've had a successful day. Do they know what it takes to have produced a good result for the company? If they struggle to answer this question, it's time to get more specific about what's expected.

However you choose to approach performance reviews, documentation establishes clear roles and responsibilities. If these responsibilities are reviewed regularly – and you can leave it to the judgment of each supervisor to decide if "regularly" means meeting daily, weekly or monthly with their staff – there should be no surprises.

The process of gaining commitment and putting it in writing ensures that everyone is aligned and on board with the ultimate goal.

Continue to devote a portion of your bi-weekly, two-hour accountability meetings to ensuring that individual and departmental performance is tracking. Encourage your leadership team to meet as often as they see fit to monitor and measure their respective departmental performance as well as individual performance in their business unit. Group goals are important, and so are individual goals. Gaining individual commitment on personal performance objectives is the next step in driving implementation and being clear on who's accountable for what.

Commitment counts because it's the contract established between a supervisor and employee.

Take Action

Review your existing process for establishing and measuring individual performance in your organization. Is the process satisfactory or can it be improved? If you currently do not have a process that provides your employees clarity about their individual role, objectives and performance measurement, make the commitment to develop this process. Write the specific action you will take with a deadline for completing it.

_____

_____

_____

_____

Establishing Consequences

"Everybody, sooner or later, sits down to a banquet of consequences."

~ Robert Louis Stevenson

Resolution on issues related to consequences of performance and accountability was deferred at the end of the planning session, and again in your first post-planning accountability meeting.

Now is the time to establish consequences.

In Chapter 9, we touched on consequences and the notion that a consequence has come to be viewed negatively when in fact a consequence is simply the result of an action. I believe that most people want to do a good job because there's a sense of accomplishment and pride in a job that's been done well.

But they need a framework by which all team members can measure the work that's being done.

You've already taken steps to provide that framework, and the feedback step discussed in the preceding section of this chapter provides a mechanism for leaders to help their staff replicate successes and eliminate failures. Your vision, goals and objectives help keep your team's internal fires stoked and give them something to strive toward because most people want to work for a cause that's bigger than themselves.

People that want to work effectively have nothing to fear from measurement. Only those who do not want to perform should worry about the new scrutiny you and your team will be bringing to their performance.

You and your leadership team must consider the rewards – and it's usually more than money (though money is important) – you will bestow in recognition of successfully completing a project, milestone or annual objective. People want to believe what they're doing matters, and when they perform well they want to be recognized. They want to matter. They want to belong to an organization that cares about the value they help the company deliver. I've watched veteran employees get misty-eyed and choked up when they receive a commendation in front of their peers. Recognition works.

You must also consider how you will deal with those who – for whatever reason – consistently fail to perform as agreed. You must strip away excuses and deal with reality. Keep emotion out of it and stick to the facts. Individual performance objectives – complete with standards for work quality, output and deadlines – provide the basis of your assessment. Decide how much time and how many chances you're going to give people to get better. But when that time is up, if it's clear they're not contributing at the desired level, you must make a change. When objectives aren't met, non-performers must go. It's not fair to the rest of the team.

When stars see that sub-par performance is tolerated, they will ask themselves why they continue working so diligently to meet their own commitments. I've seen instances where the stars are asked to take on work not being performed by laggards or to fix work that is performed incorrectly. Not only are such practices unfair, they're demoralizing. Your inability to address under-performers will create resentment among your top performers and will eventually drive them away from your organization.

Here are some questions to help you establish the consequences for performance:

- What consequences, if any, do we currently have in place?

- Do we apply those consequences consistently? If no, why not?

- What new consequences must we establish?

- Who can we learn from?

- What existing consequences must we change or eliminate?

- Am I willing to back up my promises with tangible evidence of my commitment?

- How did we celebrate our company's last major achievement?

How you handle both your stars and your laggards will be reflected in the respect your team pays you.

The consequences you establish and enforce consistently will not guarantee that the plan you are implementing will succeed in the short term or even over a sustained time period. But they will improve your odds of success.

Take Action

Review your existing process for establishing and measuring individual performance in your organization. Is the process satisfactory or can it be improved? If you currently do not have a process that provides your employees with clarity about their individual role, objectives and performance measurement, make the commitment to develop this process. Write the specific action you will take with a deadline for completing it.

_____

_____

_____

_____

Replicating Success

*"Do not let what you cannot do interfere with what you
can do."*

~ John Wooden

Every company has success stories.

What are yours?

The accountability documentation you are in the process
of developing or fine-tuning will help you pinpoint your successes in the course of a project, month, quarter or year. This
documentation can prompt discussions about performance
and value with internal and external clients as well as with employees.

Do you let your customers or clients know the steps you
take to deliver your product or service? If you don't, chances
are good they'll take those things for granted. You may not be
able to charge for any much less all of the ways in which you
provide value. But you should look for opportunities to communicate to customers the value you provide or they will not
fully appreciate the value you are delivering.

Do employees that discover faster, better, cheaper or more
predictable ways of delivering a result share their learning
with colleagues? If you have not established a system for sharing this type of valuable information, you're forcing each employee to reinvent the wheel each time he or she approaches
a particular situation as they search for their own methods of
effective performance. Ask yourself *Does our culture encourage
and reward teamwork?* An operating environment that balances
individual performance and organizational efficiency can produce consistently high levels of performance.

As part of your monitoring and measurement process,
make sure there are systems and procedures in place to identify, study and replicate your successes.

You must know which systems are working and which ones
aren't. Which employees are performing and which ones aren't.

Which suppliers are meeting your standards and which ones aren't. Which customers are profitable and which ones aren't.

Establishing systems that harness and share the information you gather from your monitoring and measuring processes is another way you can increase individual and organizational effectiveness.

Take Action

List the most significant successes your company has achieved in the last 6 – 12 months.

1. _____

2. _____

3. _____

4. _____

5. _____

What systems or procedures are in place to replicate these successes? If there currently is no system in place to replicate the success, commit now to creating one. If a system or procedure exists, ask *How can it be improved?* List one improvement you would like to see that can increase your effectiveness and consistency in areas that are already solid. Establish a deadline for completing this action.

_____

_____

_____

_____

Removing Obstacles

"Inside the ring or out, ain't nothin' wrong with going down. It's stayin' down that's wrong."

~ Muhammad Ali

There will be times when it seems as though nothing is going according to your plan.

When adversity strikes, you have two responses. You can either view yourself as a victim and succumb to the adversity, or you can adjust your plan, learn from the situation and continue moving toward your objective. It takes courage and discipline to keep going.

To answer the questions *What must we change?* and *What are we going to do?*, you must first answer the question *What exactly is the issue that we're grappling with?*

There are a variety of approaches that will help you and your team reach the heart of the matter in order to develop a solution to the problem that's got you stuck. These approaches share a diagnostic process – more questions – to help you drill down to discover the essence of the *real* problem.

Remember, the exercise you and your team used to discover or fine tune your competitive advantage? Go back to Chapter 7 and review The Five Why's. Recall that this exercise takes its name from the practice of asking – five times – why a failure has occurred or a belief is held in order to drill down to the root cause or causes of a problem, opportunity or issue.

Are your sales suffering because your prices are too high (as most sales people are inclined to believe), or is it because your value proposition is not compelling? Is your service or manufacturing capacity maxed out because all your people are busy, or is your productivity diminished because your systems and procedures for getting work done are not efficient?

Ask The Five Why's to keep drilling down until you hit pay dirt.

I've included two more exercises that my friend John Dealey shared with me years ago. Over time, I've modified them based on feedback from CEOs who have used this exercise to get unstuck.

The first exercise is an effective approach for solving problems. It's called the dancing recipe because entries dance back and forth until a possible solution emerges.

Before you write down a single word on the chart I've provided, ask yourself these three questions:

- What dollar value do I place on this problem?

- What will be the cost to me and my company of *not* solving this problem?

- Pretend it is three years from today and your revenues have declined 30 percent, you're profits are break-even, and you've terminated one quarter of your workforce. How did this situation occur? What action could you have taken to prevent this situation? What's keeping you from taking that action now?

As you begin the first exercise, don't let the simplicity of the form trick you into minimizing its power.

Exercise

The Dancing Recipe

Date_____

What is the issue?

_____

Why is the issue significant?

_____

What is the cause of the issue?

_____

What's my ideal outcome?

_____

What are the possible solutions to achieve my ideal outcome? If I was replaced, what would a new CEO do? List at least 3 solutions; creative problem solving occurs when you list 10 possible solutions.

1. _____

2. _____

3. _____

4. _____

5. _____

6. _____

7. _____

8. _____

9. _____

10. _____

Which solution do you recommend?

_____

If the recommendation you selected were approved now, what most likely could go wrong?

_____

_____

Take Action

What action will you commit to taking? By when?

_____

_____

Make sure you're addressing the real problem, then get to work executing your solution.

Exercise

Staying Focused

Armed with a possible solution to your problem, use this form to stay focused on executing at a high level the actions you must take to get you unstuck.

A. What specific achievement(s) do you want to accomplish over the next 30/90/120 days?

1. _____

2. _____

3. _____

B. What things currently have the potential to be major energy drains in your life?

1. _____

2. _____

3. _____

4. _____

5. _____

6. _____

7. _____

C. What must you do to eliminate the drains in order to focus on your priorities?

1. _____

2. _____

3. _____

Take Action

What one thing could you do this month to bring the most value to your company?

_____

_____

Remember: CEOs play offense, not defense. Stay focused on executing high-value actions.

"Life is pretty simple: You do some stuff. Most fails. Some works. You do more of what works. If it works big, others quickly copy it. Then you do something else. The trick is the doing something else."

~ Leonardo da Vinci

12

How Can We Become Even Better?

Tastes evolve. Habits change. New expectations are set. Competition encroaches.

For leaders who are driven to sustain their companies' success, it takes more than being alert to these conditions. It takes a commitment to innovation and improvement.

Innovation and improvement come from good ideas.

But where exactly do good ideas come from? Mostly by watching, asking and listening to your customers and watching human behavior. A thorough analysis of the product category, competitive insights and consumer issues can help you understand market trends, the underlying causes of trends and influencing factors (such as governmental, environmental, regulatory, cultural and demographic changes).

Are your people trained, equipped and inspired to observe patterns, question premises and then connect the dots to give customers what they want?

Are you watching your competitors to see if they're doing something differently, better or newer than you?

Are you measuring internal performance to give yourself a clearer picture of which things aren't working and why, and what must be done to improve your situation?

Even when things are working well, there's always room for growth or improvement.

And when your initiatives are stalled or things aren't working exactly as planned, your challenge as a leader is to know when to stay the course and when to change direction. Don't worry about how a change will reflect on management. Your people will already know things aren't working and won't be surprised if you initiate changes; on the contrary, they will be surprised if you don't. Just be sure to communicate the reason for the change and the outcomes you expect from the change in direction.

Innovation and improvement are processes that blend art and science. Winning companies master these processes.

What do the best companies do? How do they do it? Why do they do it this way? Why can't we?

What can we learn from the successes and failures of others? How can we become better?

Let's take a look.

Lessons from Companies We Admire

"It is harder to keep a business great than it is to build it."
~ Thomas Watson, Sr.

As you and your team continue to work your plan, you may find that you soon have picked all of the low-hanging fruit.

Good. Make sure you take the opportunity to enjoy the fruits of your labor. Celebrate the achievement of a milestone or the completion of a major action item with your team.

Reaching higher levels of effectiveness and profitability will require more effort.

Let's examine practices that have worked well for other successful companies.

These 12 lessons are from companies that all started small. Today, they're big businesses. And they're among the most admired companies in the world. They are considered the gold standards in their industry – and beyond. Not only for what they have accomplished as organizations. But also for the leaders they have produced and their achievements of innovation, effectiveness and continuous improvement.

And, most important, for the way in which they have achieved and now sustain their success.

- Neiman Marcus – Commit to Excellence

- Mary Kay Cosmetics – Obey the Golden Rule

- Microsoft Corporation – Think Small

- The Container Store – Communicate Often

- Coca-Cola – Think Outside the Box

- Southwest Airlines – Align Corporate Goals and Individual Performance

- FedEx – Measure Everything

- Intel – Ask and Answer Hard Questions

- McDonald's – Learn Continuously

- Pepsi-Cola – Use Deadlines Wisely

- Nordstrom – Empower Your People

- Ebby Halliday Realtors – Never Give Up

While some of the lessons may seem obvious, too often the obvious is overlooked.

Neiman Marcus

Commit to Excellence

"I have the simplest tastes. I am easily satisfied with the best."

~ Stanley Marcus

To become successful and remain successful, you must accept only the best.

With an investment of $25,000, Neiman Marcus opened its doors in downtown Dallas on September 10, 1907. The founders promised customers a store offering the finest fashions in ladies' apparel with superior service. Recognizing the need for a ready-to-wear fine garment industry, Neiman Marcus designed and sold the first dress to button down the front, thus enabling women to step into a dress rather than pull it over their heads and muss their hairdo. This insight led the fledgling company to a profit in its first year of business. More important, it launched a commitment of marrying pragmatism and excellence for which the $4.39 billion company is now admired worldwide.

The future, however, looked less promising in the company's early days. By the time Herbert Marcus' son Stanley joined the family business in 1926, Neiman Marcus had survived a recession and a fire that destroyed the company's entire inventory.

Despite these setbacks, Stanley Marcus moved decisively and with remarkable prescience to meet discerning customers' growing desire for beauty, craftsmanship, quality and service. His ingenuity, fortified with a commitment to excellence, propelled the company to greater financial success and international acclaim as Neiman Marcus introduced history-making innovations that have since become retailing gold standards. Among these firsts were a weekly retail fashion show, the first bridal show, the fashion industry's pre-eminent distinguished service award and its world-famous Christmas catalog. To counter a perennial drop in mid-October sales, Neiman Marcus created "Fortnight." In 1984, the company became the first retailer to reward customers' patronage through a loyalty program.

"Is the best measurable?" Stanley Marcus asked in *Quest for the Best*. "I know of no empirical devices [to measure the best], but I believe that the best is discernable to the discriminating eye. Sometimes recognition comes slowly, but eventually the discriminating customer discovers the best and passes the word around. The magazines are full of advertisement proclaiming that their products are the best, but it is the customer who finally makes this decision."

Ever alert to "the dangers of the prosperity our business was enjoying," Marcus spoke personally with his team "to warn them of the pitfalls of success. Any business responds to leadership from the top, and if management is willing to make the effort of injecting itself, it can pretty well establish the attitudes it desires," he said. "People want and respond to inspiration, but that stimulation has to come with some frequency. It's not enough to define the goals once a year; it's necessary, by personal contact, for an organization to know that the boss is aware of what's going on."

The best companies set the bar high and then continue to raise it. You must critique your organization on a continuous basis. Because the chances are good that what worked before won't work today, much less tomorrow. The principles may still be valid, but how those principles are applied likely will require an update along with a re-commitment to be the best.

Lesson:

Your commitment to excellence must be understood by all, and that commitment must never waver. Successful companies know that "good enough" never is.

Mary Kay Cosmetics

Obey the Golden Rule

"Everyone has an invisible sign hanging from their neck saying, 'Make me feel important.' Never forget this message when working with people."

~ Mary Kay Ash

Treat people the way you want to be treated.

It's a simple principle. And a powerful one, too.

Yet it's often forgotten in the hurly burly of the business world.

As the leader, it's your job to set the standard for how people are treated. And how they treat one another. Do you have any screamers that work for you? How about people that regularly embarrass colleagues publicly? Does anyone on your team use fear as a motivator? These practices may work in the short term, but they aren't sustainable and they will drive your best employees to your competitors.

Mary Kay Ash formed Mary Kay Cosmetics in 1963 with her life savings of $5,000, the help of her 20-year-old son and a deep responsibility to treat people fairly.

The Golden Rule was her guiding philosophy and she encouraged employees and members of her independent sales force "to prioritize their lives with God first, family second and career third."

The company she founded on her strong faith and those timeless principles remains one of the greatest success stories in the history of business.

Mary Kay Cosmetics has grown to become the number two worldwide direct seller of beauty products (behind Avon) with more than 200 products in six categories sold by more than 1.6 million consultants representing the company in more than 37 countries. Worldwide sales are now well over $2 billion.

The company has been named to *Fortune*'s 100 Best Companies list.

Just remember that what goes around, comes around. What will be coming around to you?

Lesson:

Treat people the way you want to be treated.

Microsoft

Think Small

> *"In this business, by the time you realize you're in trou-
> ble, it's too late to save yourself. Unless you're running
> scared all the time, you're gone."*
>
> ~ Bill Gates

Executives at Microsoft still run the company like a start-up.

The company thinks big when it comes to its objectives. After all, it targets 100% penetration of every market it's in.

But company leaders think small – that is, they think like
entrepreneurs – about everything else.

It's their responsibility to make sure every employee believes and follows entrepreneurial practices in order to achieve
the big goals the company has set for itself.

Employees are asked *What are you going to do to increase market share?*

In this type of culture, performance matters more than office
size, working hours, apparel or putting up with practices that
aren't effective. It's all about smarts and speed and results.

So if people are no longer needed, they're fired.

If managers are not capable of doing the work of the people
that report to them, they're re-assigned.

Problems are met by solutions, not excuses.

Meetings aren't called unless a decision is required; otherwise e-mail is used to move information around the company.
Decisions at meetings are insisted upon.

Everything is measured by success – not by activity.

Microsoft has preserved traits that small companies short
on time, talent and cash depend on to produce results.

Thinking small has helped Microsoft grow to be the biggest
software company in the world.

Lesson:

Don't let success go to your head; work like someone's gaining on you because they probably are.

The Container Store

Communicate Often

"Communication and leadership are the same thing."
~ Kip Tindell

Communicating may not come naturally to you. But as the leader you must do it.

As you communicate, what you say and how you say it must reflect your values and your style, otherwise you'll be perceived as insincere. When that happens, you've taken a step backward.

Kip Tindell and Garret Boone met while working at a Montgomery Ward, and along with architect John Mullen founded The Container Store in 1978 with $35,000. The trio originated the concept of a retailer of storage and organizational products.

Today, The Container Store is far and away the category leader, generating more than $600 million in 2007 sales from 41 stores. The company, which expects to open 29 new stores by 2012, has been named to *Fortune* magazine's list of "100 Best Places to Work" for eight consecutive years, beinning in 2002.

One of The Container Store's core business philosophies is that one great person equals three good people in terms of business productivity. Most employees at The Container Store are college educated and most were customers first, so communication and training are top priorities.

"Each day, we're committed to making The Container Store an even better place to work," Tindell says. "More training, benefits, communication, empowerment, FUN – it's a never-ending journey."

Communicating is hard work. Study after study shows that it's virtually impossible to over-communicate, but particularly when you're experiencing the kind of rapid growth The Container Store has enjoyed year after year.

"It takes bravery to communicate at an absurdly high level," Tindell says. "To feel like you're part of something, you must feel like you're in on everything. Over-communicating ensures that our values and standards are consistent at every store. I know that sometimes information falls into the wrong hands, but we know that most retailers can't react to it, plus it's more important to communicate everything to our employees than to sit around worrying about what the competition gets. We've made the right choice by over-communicating to all employees."

Don't let people guess what you're thinking. Tell them. Clearly. Consistently. Frequently.

Your people will reward you with effective performance and loyalty.

Lesson:

Information is power, and information that's well communicated is a powerful motivator to those important to you.

Coca-Cola

Change the Game

"We're going to take risks. What has always been will not necessarily always be forever."

~ Roberto Goizueta

When Roberto Goizueta became president of The Coca-Cola Company, the soft drink business was, as it still is today, fiercely competitive.

The Coca-Cola Company was well into its second century of existence when Goizueta took the reins. The company had grown from its beginnings in 1886 Atlanta, Georgia, in Jacobs' Pharmacy to claim in 1980 about one-third of what was considered a mature U.S. soft drink market. Any growth that was achieved tended to be measured in tenths of percentage points.

But Goizueta did not believe the market was mature.

"What," he famously asked his executives during a strategic planning session, "is the average per-capita daily consumption of fluids by the world's 4.4 billion people?"

That first question alone should have alerted the executives that Goizueta was approaching the problem from a new and completely different perspective. His executives said the answer to his question was 64 ounces.

"What," Goizueta then asked, "is the daily per-capita consumption of Coca-Cola?"

Less than two ounces, he was told.

Finally, Goizueta wanted to know Coca-Cola's worldwide "market share of the stomach."

The company's impact here was negligible.

In the hard-fought cola wars, Coca-Cola had viewed Pepsi as the enemy. Goizueta helped the company's leaders reframe the battle for the "share of the stomach" in terms of water, coffee, juice, milk and tea.

With a series of fundamentally simple questions to his key executives, Goizueta changed the game for Coca-Cola by effectively changing the category.

How can you change your game?

Lesson:

Approaching a situation from a new perspective can produce new and better results.

Southwest Airlines

Align Company Goals and Personal Performance

"We have a strategy – it's called doing."
~ Herb Kelleher

Goal-setting is top down. Goal-getting is bottom up.

So when companies and their employees are aligned on what must be done, by when and by whom, effectiveness and profitability follow.

Southwest Airlines uses its annual planning process to identify new ways to make itself better.

Each year, the company identifies between one and three corporate goals and each goal cascades down to departments that develop their respective strategies, action items, and budgets. The departmental goals cascade down to the 33,000 employees responsible for supporting the airline that has become the nation's largest domestc air carrier with 3,300 flights each day serving 64 cities in 32 states.

Southwest Airlines wasn't always a $9 billion business. Herb Kelleher led a four-year legal battle resulting in the fledgling airline's launch on June 18, 1971, with just three airplanes.

Kelleher is known as a highly focused business person with a relentless passion for delivering a quality product. Goals are established, buy-in achieved, and expectations must be met. Industry observers note that Kelleher may laugh and joke with you, but if the job you told him you handled wasn't completed, out the door you go.

The attitude of individual accountability begun 40 years ago by Kelleher is still very much a part of the company's consistent winning performance.

Today, quarterly meetings are held to determine how departmental performance – not just costs – is tracking. Group goals are important, and so are individual goals. Southwest conducts annual written performance reviews with lots of coaching in between. "We take a really hard look at the first six months of employment," says senior vice president Ginger Hardage. "We're not rack 'em and stack 'em like some companies – we give people lots of time to get better. But if it's clear they're not contributing, we make a change."

This type of planning, alignment and performance has made Southwest Airlines tops in customer satisfaction and a high-flier on Wall Street with more than three decades of consecutive profitability.

Make sure your corporate goals are aligned with the performance objectives of each individual in your organization. You can have fun and still get things done.

Lesson:

To maximize corporate performance, align your employees' performance objectives with your corporate goals.

FedEx

Measure Everything

"We make it very clear to everybody what they need to do every day. We manage the continuous improvement in a mathematical manner every single day. Our service gets better each year."

~ Fred Smith

Remember that what gets measured gets done.

FedEx is an organization obsessed with customer service and focused on tracking it.

The company was founded by Fred Smith and began operating on April 17, 1973, with 14 aircraft connecting 25 U.S. cities. Today, FedEx provides time-definite shipping to more than 220 countries and territories.

A big part of the success of FedEx is built on a foundation of measuring everything with special attention paid to speed, reliability and cost. My friend Keith Martino, a former worldwide sales manager at FedEx whose team was twice recognized as the top global accounts group in the world, says the entire organization is focused on executing against Quality Service Indicators that track 12 key areas of business performance.

These indicators include specific customer service areas such as "friendliness," "cleanliness of retail locations" and, of course "timeliness." Each of these 12 areas is further refined to measure specific performance. The area of "timeliness," for instance, breaks down into categories such as "same-day late" (an afternoon versus morning measurement that helps pinpoint breakdowns at the local level) and "wrong-day late" (which can help FedEx focus on problems occurring further upstream at the airline level).

It's this measurement system that helps maintain superb levels of business performance and, as a result, extremely satisfied customers. The company continues to fine-tune its customer satisfaction measurement systems "to be sure we take into account everything customers feel is important in creating an exceptional relationship with FedEx."

Business unit, departmental and individual plans are based on the overall corporate plan. These plans are reviewed as often as the team leaders believe they need to be – for some it's daily, for other it's weekly, for others it may be monthly. The plans are then formally reviewed for payout on an annual basis. Individuals that achieve their objectives receive bonuses and opportunities for advancement. Those that don't meet their objectives receive no bonuses and are graded down – a rarity at FedEx because "everyone is focused on hitting their objectives."

Whether you are responsible for sustaining high levels of performance or increasing performance as an organization rebuilds, measurement is key.

Lesson:

If it's important, measure it.

Intel

Ask and Answer Hard Questions

"Only the paranoid survive."

~ Andy Grove

When the future of your company is on the line, you can stay the course and try to ride out the threat. Or you can make a courageous decision that, in hindsight, is often less risky than maintaining the status quo.

At Intel in the mid-1980s, the memory chip business the company had perfected was being assaulted by Japanese competitors that had mastered the production process and were now offering chips at much lower prices than those of Intel's.

Chairman Andy Grove and co-founder Gordon Moore studied and debated options ranging from building new plants to developing new versions of chips with special-purpose memories. These options, however, weren't viable alternatives to countering the growing Japanese threat. "We had lost our bearings," Grove says. "We were wandering in the valley of death."

But in 1985, Grove and Moore made a courageous decision: abandon the memory chip business and focus on microprocessors.

Here's how it happened. Grove asked Moore, "If we got kicked out and the board brought in a new CEO, what do you think he would do?" Moore's immediate reply: "He would get us out of memories."

Grove stared at him, then said, "Why shouldn't you and I walk out the door, come back in, and do it ourselves?"

And that's exactly what Grove and Moore did.

By removing themselves from the emotional baggage of a business headed for a commodities battleground and recognizing the opportunity being created by the market, Grove and Moore asked and answered the hard question.

Their courageous decision caused the company to break with a plan that was working and fix its future on a market that ultimately has made the company even more valuable.

Andy Grove's hard question – "What would new management do?" – is a powerful tool you can use to help you frame, make and implement courageous decisions.

Lesson:

Resolve difficult issues by asking and answering key questions as though you were an outsider with a vested interest in your company's effective performance.

McDonald's

Learn Continuously

"If you think training is expensive, try ignorance."

~ Ray Kroc

Continuous learning is most potent when it's viewed as an enterprise-wide responsibility and not simply a function confined to the R&D department.

Money-making and money-saving ideas can be taught and harvested at all levels of your organization. The trick is creating an environment where learning occurs not once or occasionally, but, well, continuously.

Some companies take continuous learning to new heights. McDonald's is a pioneer.

In 1954, at age 52, Ray Kroc was selling a milk shake mixer called the Multimixer. When he saw eight Multimixers running at a single hamburger stand called McDonald's, he'd never seen so many people served so quickly. He pitched the idea of becoming the exclusive Multimixer distributor and opening several restaurants. Kroc mortgaged his home and invested his life savings to open the Des Plaines, Illinois restaurant in 1955. He made $366.12 his first day.

Six years later, the little company founded Hamburger University in the basement of a McDonald's restaurant in Illinois with a commitment to "consistent restaurant operations procedures, service, quality and cleanliness." On February 24, 1961, Hamburger University's first class of 14 students graduated.

Today, McDonald's operates 30,000 restaurants in 119 countries, serving 52 million people each day. And Hamburger University, with 19 full-time professors with restaurant operations expertise, is the learning center for more than 5,000 students each year.

McDonald's training mission is "to be the best talent developer of people with the most committed individuals to Quality, Service, Cleanliness and Value (QSC&V) in the world." Hamburger University is the company's global center of excellence for operations training and leadership development, and the curriculum uses a combination of classroom instruction, hands-on lab activities, goal-based scenarios and computer e-learning modules.

McDonald's employees align training with their specific career paths, including development paths for crew, restaurant managers, mid-managers and executives. And since 1961, more than 80,000 restaurant managers, mid-managers and owner-operators have graduated from Hamburger University.

The commitment to training is a cornerstone of the company's success.

If you consider your people your most important asset, then you'll agree that helping them be their best makes sense.

Lesson:

Train and equip your people continuously to help them help you and your company reach its full potential.

Pepsi-Cola

Use Deadlines Wisely

"It staggers me that being nice is seen as being inconsistent with being tough."

~ Craig Weatherup

Some companies are better at responding to threats than opportunities. So creating a crisis can be a necessary wake-up call for organizations that have grown rich, happy and complacent.

To say that a crisis is "created" is an overstatement since a leader's credibility is lost if the crisis isn't real. But the idea is to focus on an area of a successful company's business to demonstrate that radical change must occur within a specific timeframe if the company is to survive an emerging threat.

Threats usually fall into one of three categories: financial, customer-related or industry driven, including regulatory matters.

Some years ago, Craig Weatherup was leading Pepsi-Cola's profitable $7 billion soft drink division. He feared that a business-as-usual approach in the highly competitive industry would not be enough to secure the company's success in the years ahead. So he created a financial crisis.

In meetings with his direct reports, he set a 15% profit target versus the 10% profit target his managers were accustomed to hitting and shared feedback from some of Pepsi-Cola's most important customers about areas of frustration.

To drive the change he sought, Weatherup gave each of his lieutenants 90 days to go to school on their own operations and their customers to determine areas where the company could better serve customers while increasing profitability.

The lieutenants used the data and knowledge they gathered to train the next layer of management. And so on and so on, ultimately reaching some 30,000 employees.

As a result of this initiative, Pepsi-Cola re-organized itself into 107 units that are closer to the customer and focused on producing results at that level. Three years later, profits for the first quarter rose 22% – more than double previously acceptable profit levels.

Pepsi-Cola used a deadline to improve financial results.

Lesson:

Use short-term deadlines selectively to create a sense of urgency, accelerate change and achieve bold objectives.

Nordstrom

Empower Your People

"The only thing we have going for us is the way we take care of our customers, and the people who take care of the customers are on the floor."

~ Ray Johnson

The difference between leaders and laggards comes down to people.

Not just at the top, though that's where a company's employees take their cues.

Most companies – even manufacturers – rely on their employees to be difference-makers. That's because the products most companies sell are commodities. There's another one just like yours down the street or on the web.

So the easier it is for your customers to buy a product and the more pleasant you make the experience, the more likely it is that they will continue to buy from you. This premise, of course, assumes you're providing a quality product.

Nordstrom, Inc. was started in 1901 by two Swedish immigrants as a single shoe store in Seattle. On their first day of business, John W. Nordstrom and Carl Walin sold $12.50 in shoes. From those origins, the family-run enterprise has expanded into a 180-outlet, 27-state chain, generating annual sales approaching $7 billion.

Today, the company is organized as an inverted pyramid. Ray Johnson and other descendants of the founder recognize that sales associates are the organization's closest link to its customers. All functions of Nordstrom are organized to support the sales staff. Employees are given great latitude in solving customers' problems. This practice clearly delivers results: The firm maintains the highest sales per square foot of retail space ratios in the industry, nearly twice those of other department stores.

How can you raise the level of service you're now providing your customers? Have you fully empowered your employees to give your customers what they're expecting from you?

When you acknowledge that customers drive your business and not the other way around, you can keep bureaucratic red-tape to a minimum, keep your workforce focused and motivated, and keep your customers happy and coming back for more – even in tough times.

Lesson:

Trust your employees and give them the freedom to do what it takes to keep your customers satisfied.

Ebby Halliday Realtors

Never Give Up

*"When you develop an ethic where if you don't work, you
don't eat, you have a leg up on anything else that happens
in your life."*

~ Ebby Halliday

By whatever name you choose to call it – persistence or passion, stubbornness or stamina, drive or determination – all
great leaders demonstrate the will to win. They refuse to give
up.

Ebbiday Halliday worked her way through high school in
Kansas and developed her work ethic in those years. She graduated in 1929, the year every bank in America closed because of
the Great Depression. Halliday did not lose heart, but moved
to Dallas in 1938 and continued to work. In 1945, her persistence was rewarded when she started her real estate company
with $12,000 of her own money.

"The market has been up and down in our 63 years in business," she says "but we've been resilient. When you're down,
you can't always try to score a touchdown. You have to make
a first down. Then another one, and another one, and another
one. If you make enough first downs, you'll eventually score
your touchdown. The important thing is to not give up."

In the 1960s, Halliday once paid out "every cent" she saved
to her employees. She persistently worked through it.

In the 1980s when the Texas real estate market had again
gone south, Halliday divested her real estate portfolio to keep
the company going. She persistently worked through it.

Today, Ebby Halliday Realtors is the biggest independent
firm of its type in Texas and the 19th largest nationwide. Ebby
Halliday Realtors operates 30 offices with more than 1,600 li-
censed associates. Its web traffic averages more than 22,000 hits

per day. And in 2006, Ebby Haliday Realtors recorded $4.7 billion in sales volume, marking the best year in the company's rich history.

At some point as you and your team are working through tough issues, a fresh wave of doubt and problems will confront you as you near the completion of your goal. Don't be surprised. Don't be surprised if things that have never gone wrong before now go wrong. Don't be surprised if that is the occasion when critics begin to knock the project. Don't be surprised if your passion for the work suddenly evaporates. Just don't give up.

Lesson:

Persistence pays. Never give up.

Exercise

Turning Thoughts into Action

> *"We should be taught not to wait for inspiration to start a thing. Action always generates inspiration. Inspiration seldom generates action."*
>
> ~ Frank Tibolt

You've taken a quick look at ways 12 much-admired companies have created, built and sustained their success.

Answer these four questions right now to turn your thoughts into action.

What lesson hit you the hardest?

_____

_____

Why?

_____

_____

What actions will you commit to take to apply a lesson to improving your company's effectiveness? List a deadline for completing this action.

1. _____

2. _____

3. _____

4. _____

5. _____

6. _____

For what expected outcome?

_____

_____

Flexibility and Adaptability

"It is not the strongest of the species that survive, nor the most intelligent; it is the one that is most adaptable to change."

~ Charles Darwin

From the pre-Cambrian swamps Darwin studied to today's climate of change, confusion and uncertainty, the maxims are the same. Stay alive, adapt and execute your plan.

Your first responsibility in this survival of the fittest environment is to keep your company alive through honest means. Ultimately, however, your primary objective is to thrive by keeping yourself, your employees and your company moving toward higher ground.

By increasing your effectiveness, you increase your value to customers. And by increasing your value to customers, you increase their loyalty to your company. Customer loyalty drives company sustainability.

It's a cycle. One that will reward those who adapt. And one that will punish those that do not.

You therefore must live your plan every day. You must stay alert. You must expect the unexpected as you move toward your potential. You must be intentional. And you must be urgent.

You will be tested every day.

So continue to constantly monitor, measure and critique yourself and those you work with. What worked before may not work today. Don't become so fixed in your patterns that you lose sight of your vision and forget your original objectives.

As you and your team continue meeting twice a month in your two-hour accountability meetings, you should expect to have completed most if not all of the action items from your two-day planning session as you reach the five-, six, or seven-month mark. Every organization will reach this stage at a different point in time.

When you do – whether it's 150 days or seven months after you begin executing your plan – it will be appropriate to reassemble your leadership team in an all-day, eight-hour meeting. Why do this? Why not continue holding the accountability meetings? Those are working well, you might say.

There are at least four reasons to invest this time together:

1. **Celebrate as a leadership team your accomplishments thus far** – Celebrations are important because they acknowledge short-term successes and refresh minds, bodies and spirits for the next step on your goal-getting journey.

2. **Assess your performance** – While you're doing this on a bi-weekly basis, the structure of your accountability meetings do not allow you to invest time as a leadership team discussing what's working and what isn't. Re-assess your performance using the diagnostic tool from the initial two-day planning session. Compare your two sets of scores. Use this eight-hour block of time together to review your original Migration Plan from your first planning session. What's changed? What continues to apply?

3. **Look to the future** – Based on the discussion that occurs in your update session about what is and isn't working and your review of your original Migration Plan, decide as a group where you will stay the course and where you will adapt.

4. **Recalibrate your plan** – Your plan should be a living, breathing document, so make changes to your existing plan that are necessary, establish new action items and commit them to writing

Revisit some of the questions that were posed in your first two-day planning meeting. Here are some others for you and your team to address:

- What changes have occurred that we did not anticipate? What changes occurred that we over- or underestimated?

- How have these changes affected the priorities we established in our first planning meeting?

- How do the scores on this assessment compare to the scores on our initial assessment? Where did we improve? Where did we not? Why?

- What business practices must we adapt, continue or eliminate as a result of these changes?

- Are we saying and doing the things that our people need to hear and see to believe in what the company is doing, and to give their best efforts to help us get there?

- Are our improvement initiatives linked to our most strategic issues? To what our customers value most?

- Are we doing the right things right, or simply doing things right?

- How does our vision look from this vantage point? Has it changed? Should it be bigger and bolder?

Once you've adapted your existing plan and committed new action items to writing, bring out your original Pledge of Accountability at the end of your eight-hour session. Read the Pledge. Then ask everyone to re-commit to it.

As you adjourn the session, remind your leaders that real change occurs over time. Significant progress has been achieved. But it should be clear to all from the plan that's been adapted that we can continue to get even better.

At this point, you will have invested the majority of your 73 hours – somewhere between 40 and 50 hours – in the development and implementation of your company's plan.

Next week, you will resume your bi-weekly two-hour accountability meetings.

Continue to focus your time on those vital, strategic activities that push your company forward to new levels of effectiveness and profitability. You will adapt your practices while hanging on tightly to your values.

And when another year rolls around, you will bring your team together once again for another two-day planning session as you continue along your path to winning.

The line that separates successful companies from those that habitually under-perform or fail altogether is such a fine one that leaders, as Darwin suggests, may miss seeing it "until the hand of time reveals it."

What Does Winning Mean to You?

> *"There is an immutable conflict at work in life and in business, a constant battle between peace and chaos. Neither can be mastered, but both can be influenced. How you go about that is the key to success."*
>
> ~ Philip Knight

Winning means different things to different people.

I won't try to tell you what winning should mean to you.

But my experience is that, often times, leaders find themselves in a position where their business goals and personal goals are not congruent. Simply stated, their two sets of goals are out of whack with one another.

Most business leaders aspire to their positions because they're skilled, hard-working and they envision a better life for themselves. More freedom. More personal satisfaction. More of the good life. Their natural abilities and passion to succeed help make them winners on a small scale.

As their responsibility grows, some leaders gradually discover that they're working harder than ever. They may have some nice grown-up toys and they're still in charge, but they often find they're spending more time away from their personal pursuits of happiness than they would like. Unexpected personal challenges surface. Work-life balance is a joke. The idea of a "better life" is an elusive goal.

Does this description strike a familiar note with you? Could it be you in a few more years?

Then answer these two questions:

What do I want out of life?
Is my business helping me get it or keeping me from it?

Make a list of personal goals that define winning on your terms.

Here's a goal-setting approach I developed for the CEO group I lead to help busy leaders remember that a business goal is simply one of several goals comprising a fulfilling life. I call it "The 7 Fs," and the exercise prompts you to consider what these seven significant life categories will look like in a year (or whatever time period you wish to assign):

Family
Friends
Faith
Fitness

Financial
Function (career)
Fun

The complete exercise is shown in the Appendix.

Compare your list of personal goals with the goals you've established for your business. How do these two sets of goals complement one another? Where are they out of alignment?

Will your business – on its current trajectory – help you achieve your personal goals? If so, congratulations. Stay the course.

If not, ask yourself what changes must occur in order to get you to where you want to go.

"Twenty years from now," wrote Mark Twain about the human condition, "you will be more disappointed by the things you didn't do than by the ones you did. So throw off the bow lines, sail away from this safe harbor, catch the trade winds in your sails. Explore, dream, disover."

In other words, chart a course to win.

Appendix

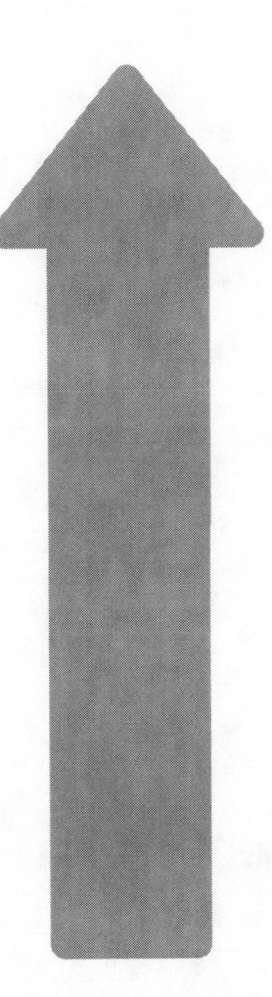

*Give us the tools
and we will finish the job.*

~ Winston Churchill

More Tools

Sample Invitation to Planning Meeting

To: All planning session participants

From: CEO

I'd like to invite you to join me and the other senior leaders of [name of company] for a two-day planning session on [dates].

We're holding this planning session in order to evaluate the past year and to begin thinking about ways to build on our strengths and focus on areas where we'd like to be stronger next year. We've retained an outside facilitator to guide us through the planning process.

Our two-day planning session will be held at [name of facility]. For those joining us from out of town, we've already made reservations for you at [nearby hotel/same facility], but you'll need to arrange your own travel. We'll plan to have a team dinner the evening following the first day's planning session, so please note that on your calendar as well.

There's nothing for you to prepare or do in advance of our planning. Just bring an open mind and a willingness to think about ways we can build on our past success.

I look forward to being with you at this important company event.

Sample Agenda for
Two-Day Planning Meeting

<u>First day</u>

■ Opening remarks by CEO
  ➤ The importance of planning
  ➤ Expected outcomes
  ➤ S.M.A.R.T. goals exercise

■ Introduction of the facilitator
  ➤ Establishing clubhouse rules
  ➤ Assessment
  ➤ Problem-solving exercise

■ Reflections & Celebrations
  ➤ Biggest accomplishment
  ➤ Biggest disappointment
  ➤ What do you want to celebrate one year from today?

■ Small group exercise
  ➤ What's working? Why?
  ➤ What's not working? Why?
  ➤ What is our profit? What should it be?

■ Who Are You? Identity Pyramid

■ BREAK FOLLOWED BY WORKING LUNCH

■ Small group exercise: Articulating your competitive advantage

■ BREAK

■ CEO's Vision

■ Small group exercise: Articulating your Vision

- Feedback on first day's session

- ADJOURN TO HAPPY HOUR/GROUP DINNER

<u>Second day</u>

- Review accomplishments of first day

- Exercise: Start/Stop
  - ➢ Establish accountability partners
  - ➢ Review time management systems

- Small group exercise: Determining priorities
  - ➢ Report back to entire group
  - ➢ Achieve consensus on priorities

- BREAK

- Small group exercise: Complete Migration Plan
  - ➢ Report back to entire group
  - ➢ Achieve consensus on general direction

- BREAK FOLLOWED BY LUNCH

- Small group exercise: Develop Action Plan
  - ➢ Report back to entire group
  - ➢ Achieve consensus on action plan to be implemented
  - ➢ Schedule bi-weekly accountability meetings
  - ➢ Ask for volunteer/Assign responsibility to transcribe meeting notes

- Pledge of Accountability

- Feedback on second day's session

- ADJOURN

Sample Memo to Non-Participants

To: Non-planning session participants

From: CEO

We will be holding an off-site strategic planning meeting for [company name] on [date].

In a perfect world, all of you would attend the two-day meeting.

Unfortunately, our business demands are such that we cannot afford to have you away from the office for the two-day meeting.

It is important that we get your input. Thus, you can expect a call from [name of facilitator] prior to the meeting. [Name of facilitator] will be leading us through the meeting. He/She will also present your comments, though he/she will not attribute any of your comments to you or anyone.

Everything you tell him/her will be treated confidentially so that no one will know who is saying what. What's important is that we receive your candid assessment about our organization. So please be open and honest with him/her.

We are holding this planning session in order to evaluate [last year] and to begin thinking about ways to build on our strengths and focus on areas where we would like to be stronger [this year]. There is nothing for you to prepare or do in advance of [name of facilitator]'s call.

Thanks in advance for your input and for all that you do for [company name].

Questions for Non-Participants

Phone script for facilitator: You should be aware from [CEO name]'s email/memo that the company is holding a planning meeting on [date]. Given time and space limitations as well as the need to continue operations and take good care of customers, not everyone can attend this meeting. But your input is important, and we want to get your input on key areas of the [company name]'s operation.

Everything that you say will be held in confidence. No comments will be attributed to you or any person. Your comments and those of other people will be presented to illustrate patterns of strengths and weaknesses as well as opportunities and threats facing the organization.

1. What's your role in the organization?

2. What's working? What's isn't?

3. What's your biggest opportunity? What's your biggest threat or obstacle? [If the person asks "Me personally or the company?" ask them to answer both ways.]

4. If you could change one thing what would it be?

5. What one thing could the company do to make you more successful?

These questions are broad, overly simplistic and open-ended in order to allow people not attending the planning session the opportunity to speak about a range of topics. As with other simple methods, do not discount their power and effectiveness at uncovering or confirming areas that pose significant opportunities for or problems to the organization. These questions may lead to other questions that could be asked based on the initial response. The survey provides tangible proof that the organization values this person's input.

Mental Traits to Consider

In *The Thinker's Toolkit* by former CIA analyst Morgan Jones, seven key mental traits are discussed that "have the greatest adverse effects on our ability to analyze and solve problems." The seven are:

1. There is an emotional dimension to almost every thought we have and every decision we make.

2. Mental shortcuts our unconscious minds continuously take influence our conscious thinking.

3. We are driven to view the world around us in patterns.

4. We instinctively rely on, and are susceptible to, biases and assumptions.

5. We feel the need to find explanations for everything, regardless of whether the explanations are accurate.

6. Humans have a penchant to seek out and put stock in evidence that supports their beliefs and judgments while eschewing and devaluing evidence that does not.

7. We tend to cling to untrue beliefs in the face of contradictory evidence.

Jones goes on to offer this riddle:

The new chief executive, one of the youngest in his nation's history, is being sworn into office on a bleak, cold, cloudy day in January. Standing beside him is his predecessor, a military leader who had led the nation through a world war. The new chief executive was raised as a Catholic and rose to his new position in part because of his vibrant charisma. He is revered by the people and will play a critical role in a military crisis that will face his nation. His name will become legendary.

Jones writes that nearly every American believes it refers to John F. Kennedy with former World War II general and, later, president Dwight Eisenhower standing by his side.

But the other person that Jones says he "has in mind" is Adolph Hitler, standing beside President Paul von Hindenburg, who led Germany through World War I.

Jones notes that as the evidence to support our initial judgment mounts, "we are disinclined to consider other alternatives."

The lesson:

Keep an open mind.

The Power of an Open Mind

Question 1

If you knew a woman who was pregnant, had eight children already and of these eight, three were deaf, two were blind, one was mentally retarded, and she had syphilis, would you recommend that she have an abortion?

Question 2

It is time to elect a new world leader and your vote will decide the election.

Here are the facts about the three candidates:

Candidate A
He associates with crooked politicians and consults with an astrologist. He's had two mistresses. He also chain smokes and drinks eight to 10 martinis a day.

Candidate B
He was kicked out of office twice, sleeps until noon, used opium in college and drinks a quart of whiskey every evening.

Candidate C
He was a decorated war hero. He's a dedicated vegetarian, doesn't drink, doesn't smoke and has never cheated on his wife.

Which of these three candidates is your choice?

Answer to Question 1

If you said "yes" you killed Ludwig von Beethoven.

Answer to Question 2

Candidate A is Franklin D. Roosevelt
Candidate B is Winston Churchill
Candidate C is Adolph Hitler

The lesson:

Be careful about jumping to conclusions.

100 Critical Questions

Over the years, we've developed four general categories of questions designed to uncover problems and opportunities that currently exist inside and outside your organization and that may exist in the future. During the planning process, we've found that it may not take asking all 100 questions or it may take asking 100 more. These 100 questions are plenty to get you started. You'll develop your own questions based on your current situation and based on the responses you get to these questions. What's important is discovering or re-discovering the hidden value that exists within every organization.

What do you want to celebrate one year from now? Three years?

1. How would you describe long-term success? What will your successful company *look* like?

2. What are your short-term corporate goals? Long-term corporate goals?

3. Are these destinations where you *want* to go or where you *expect* to go? What can be done to turn them into destinations where you want to go?

4. What's your CEO's exit strategy? What's your timeframe for exiting?

5. [For private companies] Would you characterize the company as a lifestyle company or a growth company?

6. What happens if the CEO is incapacitated? What's your succession plan?

7. What's the exit strategy for the rest of management? Their timeframe?

How would you describe your company today?

1. What business are you in? Briefly describe the history of your company. How did you come to be in the business that you are in today?

2. How do you deliver value to your customers?

3. What systems do you have in place to replicate success in the various phases of your business: talent attraction/retention/training, work product development and delivery, sales and marketing, distribution, accounting and finance?

4. Who are your customers? Who are your customers' customers?

5. What are the traits of your best customers? How can you attract more of them?

6. Which customers' needs are changing most significantly? Why? What opportunities do these changes present?

7. Do your customers sign agreements with you or do they use your product or service on an as-needed basis? What does that commitment typically mean in terms of dollars spent with you? What's the average length of a relationship? Size? What's ideal?

8. What are the personality traits of your company? Why these traits?

9. There are three characteristics of all great companies, and exceptional companies make one of these three their competitive advantage: Operational excellence, Innovation and Customization. With which do you lead?

10. How would your customers describe your company? Why?

11. What do customers and prospects like most and least

about your company? What are the barriers customers and prospects must overcome to take the action you desire? What hurdles or barriers could you remove that offer the potential to make customers major users of your products or services? What reward can you provide them for taking the action you desire?

12. Can each employee tell you what constitutes a good result that they produce each day for the company?

13. What is your unfair advantage that causes your customers to select you over your competition?

14. How do you gather customer feedback?

15. When was the last time this information was gathered? What did you learn? What changes did you make as a result of this new information? What was the outcome?

16. Do you consider your organization a market-driven organization? Sales-driven? Engineering-driven? Finance-driven? How so? Which of these disciplines puts the company most in touch with those that use your products/services?

17. What are the three most important sources of new business for you?

18. How do you address each of these new business sources within your sales and marketing process to ensure you capitalize on these opportunities?

19. Describe the each step of your sales and marketing process. What are the activities in each? How would you characterize the current effectiveness of this process?

20. Who sells in your company? Is it realistic to make everyone a salesperson for your company? If so, how? If not, why not?

21. When you lose a "sale," what is typically the reason stated by those selling?

22. In your opinion, what's the real reason you lose business opportunities?

23. What are the strengths of your sales and marketing process? Weaknesses? How can we build upon the strengths? How can we diminish weaknesses?

24. How long is your sales cycle from the time someone expresses interest in your product/service until they sign agreement to do business with you?

25. How does each step of your operation bring value to your customers? How does your operation work? If there is no value, why do you have that step?

26. What are your products/services?

27. In what situations is your company found, or its products/services found? Any surprising situations that represent an under-served opportunity? Who uses your product or service in a way that you did not intend for it to be used?

28. In what other situations would you like to be found? How can you get there?

29. Are there situations you would not like to be found where you currently exist? What are they? Are there situations or customers for whom the cost of providing a product or service are unusually high? Why are you there or providing that product or service? Should you leave that space or abandon that product or service? If so, how?

30. Describe the product development process. Describe the most recent major breakthrough made at your company in terms of product, service or process. What has been the impact of that breakthrough?

31. Are there other products or services that need to be considered? If so, why?

32. When you think about your brand – company name, logo, colors and, ultimately, the promise you're making to people who buy what your company sells, how is that brand serving you? How will that brand serve you in the future?

33. What value does the brand currently represent? What value can and should it represent in the future? How does your brand contribute or detract from the enterprise value your company is creating?

34. What are some colors that best describe your organization? Why these?

35. What are some symbols that best describe your organization? Why these?

36. What are some slogans that best describe your organization? Why these?

37. Are there any slogans you would like to be used to describe your company? Are there any current slogans, symbols or colors currently in use you'd like to eliminate? Why?

What keeps you up at night?

1. What significant events could potentially occur – internally or externally – that would make your business plan obsolete?

2. Who is the competition? Consider non-traditional sources, such as technology, culture, legislation/regulation, demographics, etc.

3. Is there a "gold standard" for companies like yours? Is there a "gold standard" outside your industry? How have these leaders addressed issues comparable to yours?

4. What are the competition's strengths? What are their weaknesses?

5. What are the most significant changes your competitors have made recently? How do those changes affect you?

6. Do they sell to the same customers as you?

7. How do you compare to your competition?

8. If you are viewed as subservient, how can you strengthen your position?

9. If you are viewed as superior or as a leader, what needs to be done to maintain this position?

10. How is your product or service different from your competitors'?

11. If it is not different, how can you become or be perceived as different?

12. What types of efforts are needed to win big?

13. What is your definition of winning big?

14. What's the worst thing that can happen to the company?

15. What are you willing to commit to in order to see your view of the future become reality?

16. What are you not willing to commit to in order to see your view of the future become reality?

If anything were possible and there were no constraints, what would you like your company to achieve?

1. What would that new organization do? What's stopping you from becoming that new organization?

2. Who would be that new company's customers?

3. What resources are necessary to accomplish this? How do you plan on securing the necessary resources?

4. Can your current organizational structure support a new direction?

5. What are the strengths of your organizational structure? How are these strengths being replicated? How is information shared inside your company?

6. Who are the stars? Laggards? How do you motivate and reward the stars? How are laggards addressed?

7. What are the weaknesses of your organizational structure? What are your gaps? Redundancies?

8. What must occur for your organization to support a new direction? Will your current culture support such a move? If so, how? If not, why not? If not, what changes to the corporate culture will need to take place?

9. Do you have the internal capabilities to accomplish these cultural changes?

10. Do you have the right people to accomplish this?

11. Are your people properly aligned operationally to accomplish this? Philosophically? Financially?

12. Are they properly equipped and trained?

13. If not, what type of people do you need? What type of training are you willing to provide?

14. Will these be additional staff members or replacements?

15. Do you have the internal capability to find these people?

16. What are your customers currently looking for?

17. What will your customers look for in the future?

18. Is a plan in place to meet those needs? If so, what is it?

19. If not, how can we prepare for these future needs?

20. How do your markets (employees, customers, prospects,

suppliers, investment community, regulatory community, recruits, media) currently view you?

21. Have you obtained feedback from them recently? If so, do you obtain feedback regularly?

22. How do you want to be seen by your markets?

23. What are your channels of distribution?

24. What other potential channels exist? Have they been explored? If so, what was the outcome?

25. What would have made the outcome a greater success?

26. If not, what would need to take place to allow you to explore these additional channels? How do they work?

27. What are the significant events occurring within your company over the next six months? Twelve months?

28. What are the noticeable dynamics that are creating important changes for your organization? What are the subtle dynamics – inside and outside your organization – that no one is watching?

29. What are the most significant trends you'd most like to capitalize on?

30. What are the dangerous waves in your industry you'd most like to avoid?

31. Where will future profitable growth come from?

32. How willing are you to change course if something is not working?

33. If change is difficult, what can be to done to make change an accepted business practice?

34. Do you measure results? If so, how? In all areas of the organization? If not, why? If not, how could result measurement become part of your business practice?

35. If you had it to do over again – let's say you were just start-ing out – what would you do differently?

36. Is there anything we've not covered that we should have covered? Is there any point you'd like to make or empha-size?

Positioning Portrait

Positioning Portrait℠

Symbols

Symbols, shapes, images and concepts that describe what the organization does and how others view it. These images can include those in use now (i.e., logos and symbols) and those to be considered for future use.

Personality

What are the animate qualities of your organization?

If your organization was a person, who would it be? Why?

What images come to mind when those inside your organization think about it?

What images come to mind when those outside the organization think about it?

Situation

Where are your products or services found?

In what situations are your products or services used?

Are there other situations where they are not currently found or used but could be found or used in the future?

Colors	Sounds	Slogans
Colors that may already be in use in logo, website, letterhead, office décor, etc.	Sounds that describe your organization.	Slogans, phrases and words that describe your organization.
Colors reflecting the organization's personality.	These sounds can include words or phrases that are often heard as well as sounds that you associate with your organization (e.g., whooping it up when an achievement occurs).	These words can include advertising headlines or taglines.
		These words can also include words or phrases that are in common use or that are being used by other companies.

Product

All of the products and services currently provided by your organization.

Value Revelation Chain

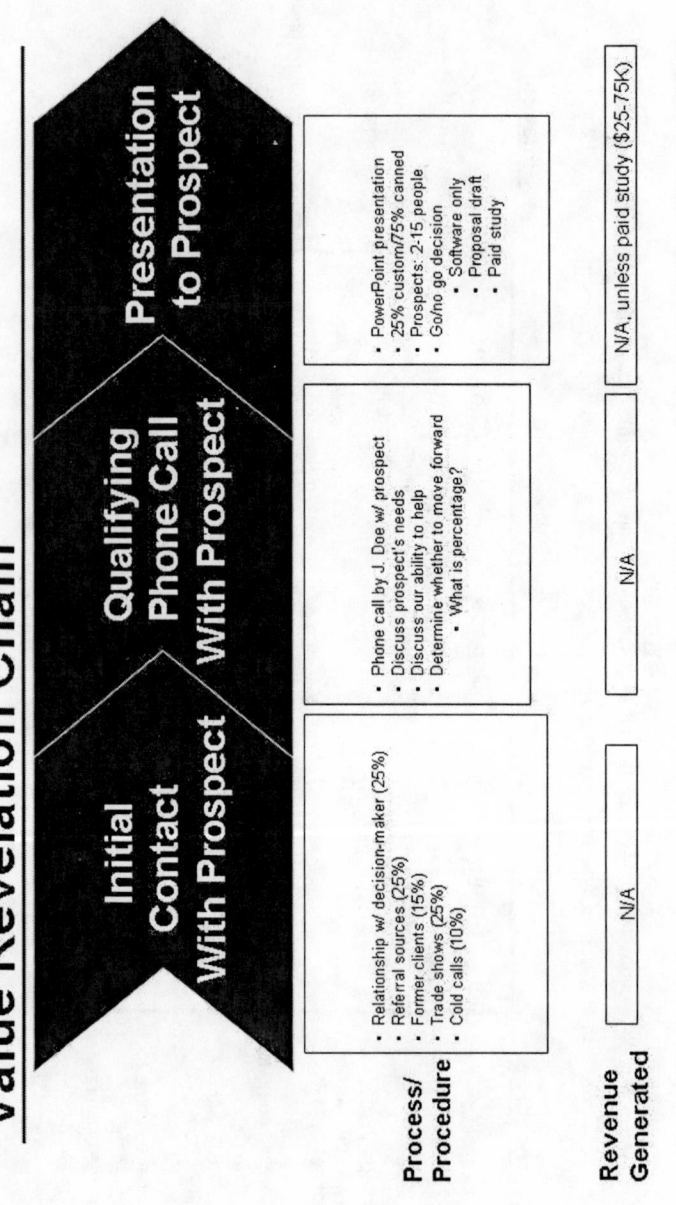

Value Revelation Chainsm

Initial Contact With Prospect

Qualifying Phone Call With Prospect

Presentation to Prospect

Process/Procedure

- Relationship w/ decision-maker (25%)
- Referral sources (25%)
- Former clients (15%)
- Trade shows (25%)
- Cold calls (10%)

- Phone call by J. Doe w/ prospect
- Discuss prospect's needs
- Discuss our ability to help
- Determine whether to move forward
  - What is percentage?

- PowerPoint presentation
- 25% custom/75% canned
- Prospects: 2-15 people
- Go/no go decision
  - Software only
  - Proposal draft
  - Paid study

Revenue Generated

| N/A | N/A | N/A, unless paid study ($25-75K) |

BUSTIN & CO.

NOTE: This chart is the first of three produced during a strategic planning exercise, though the names and figures are fictional.

Vision Waterfall®

V I S I O N

Positioning your Competitive Advantage

Priorities

Programs

Partnerships

Processes

Functional Objectives

Personal Objectives

Desired Action

Sample Migration Plan Worksheet

On the following page is a completed Migration Plan for Year 1 of an actual company. The charts for Years 2 and 3 are not included. All proprietary information has been removed and the identity of the company is confidential. Used with permission.

Year 1

	Moving from...	Moving to...
Revenue	$65,000,000	$100,000,000
Division Contribution	$500,000	$11,000,000
Employee ROA Bonus %	3%	28%
Strategic Focus	Continue excellent operating performance	Improve excellent operating performance
	Quality = 0.70% of sales	Quality = 0.80% of sales
	Detailing effectiveness = 81%	Detailing effectiveness = 90%
Major Challenges	Increase sales profitably	See revenue goals above
	589 Builders	700 Builders (20% new)
	Improve maturity of sales and sales support teams	Execution of sales growth plan; conduct sales training
Infrastructure Changes	8 DSMs	12 DSMs
	No Biz Dev coordinator	New, effective BD coordinator
Sales & Mktg Changes	Focus on price	Focus on value
	Quote rate: 15%	Quote rate: 25%

Used with permission

BUSTIN

Sample Action Plan Template

Action Plan

Objective:

Action steps	Responsibility	Due date	Status

Sample Action Plan Worksheet

Action Plan

Objective: Increase sales revenue 7% by Dec. 31

Action steps	Responsibility	Due date	Status
Evaluate existing sales process, including quotas	Tom	2/1	
Sell more existing products to existing customer base	Tom	Review monthly	
Conduct sales refresher course	Tom	2/17 – 4/2	
Sell new products to existing customers	Tom	Review monthly	
Examine new markets (product, geography, industry) for expansion	Don, Tom	3/1	
Examine, adopt industry "gold standards"	Tom, Jennifer	2/17	

Sample Pledge of Accountability

I pledge that I will faithfully execute the [company name] [year] action plan developed [date of planning session].

I will abide by [company name]'s values that we have re-confirmed at this planning session.

I will be open to change and supportive of others. I will offer comments and constructive criticism to my colleagues in a helpful, respectful manner. And I will receive others' comments with the understanding that they offer me their comments with the intention of helping me improve my effectiveness.

I agree to accept the consequences of my performance – good and bad.

I further pledge to increase my personal effectiveness and enjoyment in order to help [company name] achieve its vision of [insert vision statement].

Signed,

[each participant in the planning process]

A New Way to Think About
How You Spend Your Time

CEO versus COO

CEO – External focus	COO – Internal focus
"The buck stops here"	Day-to-day activities
Leader	Problem-solver
Strategic	Tactical
Good delegator	Detail person
Visionary	Massaging the process
Half full	Half empty
Moral compass	Follow-up
Good listener	Takes care of customers
Knowledgeable – or not	Takes care of employees
Resource allocation: people, money, priorities	Takes care of suppliers
Focused on the value of the organization	*Focused on the efficient and effective operation of the organization*

Complete the exercise on the next page to increase your personal effectiveness.

CEOs Play Offense – Not Defense

1. Take a blank piece of paper and draw a line down the middle of the page. Write "CEO" at the top of the left column and "COO" at the top of the right column.

2. Think about where you currently spend your time in your business, and using the words and phrases in each column above as guidelines, list those activities in either the CEO or the COO column. Be specific. Alternately, you may find it valuable to track your time in 30-minute increments for 30 days to get a more precise accounting of how you're spending your time.

3. Estimate the percentage of time you spend on CEO activities. Now estimate the time you spend on COO activities.

4. How much of your time is spent on CEO activities? On non-CEO activities? Is this how your time should be spent?

5. If you are spending too much of your time on non-CEO activities, what changes must you make to spend time where you are most effective?

6. List the non-CEO activities you will stop doing by delegating or eliminating. Be specific.

7. List the person to whom you will delegate these activities with a deadline for making the hand-off.

It is virtually impossible to be effective attempting to perform the duties of both the CEO and the COO. Where do you and your company receive the highest return on the use of your time?

Sample Agenda for
All-Day Planning Update Session

Date

Agenda

■ Purpose and expectations of today's session

■ Review of Clubhouse Rules established at first planning meeting

■ Self-introduction of each participant
  ➢ Hits: One significant accomplishment that I did NOT anticipate
  ➢ Misses: Most significant priority I expected to accomplish but did not

■ Re-set with self-assessment
  ➢ Post all totals, calculate average score & discuss

■ Review progress on objectives/priorities & celebration
  ➢ Rank progress on each objective (scale of 1 – 10)
  ➢ Biggest corp. achievement(s) since last annual planning session
  ➢ Biggest shortfalls in same period

■ BREAK

■ Small group exercise: What's working, what's not working & why

■ What event(s) did we NOT anticipate?
  ➢ How did we address this unanticipated event?
  ➢ How has this event(s) affected our performance?
    • Individually?
    • As a functional area?

- As a company?

- **BREAK FOLLOWED BY WORKING LUNCH**

- What's holding us back? What's propelling us forward?

- Small group exercise: Back to the future
  - ➤ Pretend it is December, and sales are flat to declining, financial targets will not be achieved, and (number) positions have been eliminated due to cost-cutting measures. Explain how and why this happened.
  - ➤ Next, determine what could have been done to prevent these cuts.
  - ➤ Finally, translate those preventative measures into revising existing priorities and objectives for the remainder of the year.

Drill down with new/more specific action item on areas where under-achieving occurs

- Finishing strong, looking ahead: Mid-year look at objectives and priorities
  - ➤ What successes can we replicate?
  - ➤ What problems can we avoid?
  - ➤ What one result would represent a pleasant surprise to your client or colleagues?
  - ➤ What new idea can you suggest to improve effectiveness in the next 90 days?
  - ➤ What tasks must we continue/improve, add and eliminate?

- Update Action Plan

- Review Pledge of Accountability and Re-Commit

- **ADJOURN**

The 7 Fs
Goal-Setting to Enhance Your Life

What's a hugely ambitious future that you passionately want to achieve for yourself or your organization that it's worth re-inventing not just your organization but your entire self?

_____

_____

_____

_____

What will these seven significant life categories look like to you one year from today:

Family_____

_____

_____

Friends_____

_____

_____

Faith _____

_____

_____

Fitness _____

_____

_____

Financial _____

_____

_____

_____

Function _____

_____

_____

_____

Fun _____

_____

_____

_____

Now select the single most important goal from one of the seven categories of goals.

Write down the category and goal: _____

_____

_____

_____

Write down how you will characterize your progress toward achieving your goal at each of these points in the coming year (What will have happened? What will you have accomplished? What will remain to be accomplished?):

March 31, (year): _____

_____

_____

_____

June 30, (year): _____

_____

_____

_____

September 30, (year): _____

_____

_____

December 31, (year): _____

_____

_____

Write down the impact of NOT achieving your goal: _____

_____

_____

_____

Write down the impact of achieving your goal: _____

_____

_____

Write down how you will feel when you achieve your goal:

_____

_____

_____

_____

_____

Index

About the Author

Greg Bustin founded Bustin & Co. in 1994 after leading the Dallas office of an international consulting firm to unprecedented levels of success. Today he consults with leadership teams in a wide range of industries and leads a think tank for successful CEOs committed to improving their performance. Bustin speaks regularly to business and nonprofit organizations. His first book, *Take Charge! How Leaders Profit From Change*, was published in 2004. Bustin has led more than 100 strategic planning sessions for leadership teams.

Printed in the United States
110293LV00003B/157-183/P

9 781587 366512